Praise for *In Our Youth*

"From a picture of twenty-nine young men standing in front of a biplane, Scully aptly describes each one. Also featured are Osborne Orr, Earl Godfrey, and George Trim, three pilots who helped build Canada's aviation industry in the 1920s and 1930s. This, plus the black and white photos of the pilots and their planes make *In Our Youth* a fascinating read."

ROGER GUNN author of *Raymond Collishaw and the Black Flight* and *Masters of the Air: The Great War Pilots McLeod, McKeever and MacLaren*

"From a single photo of twenty-nine young men in front of an aircraft in 1916, Scully teases out their respective stories: how they learned to fly, fought—and sometimes died—over French battlefields, then returned to play pioneering roles in Canadian aviation. Accessible, well researched, and fascinatingly personal."

KEITH C. OGILVIE editor of *Failed to Return: Canada's Bomber Command Sacrifice in the Second World War*

"Angus Scully takes readers on a fascinating journey into the world of Canada's Great War pilots, the young men who flew the Sopwith Camels and Handley-Pages over Germany and France. *In Our Youth* honours these heroes by telling their riveting stories."

JAMES THAYER author of *House of Eight Orchids*

"Angus Scully has created a picture of early Canadian aviation. Using a group photo of pilot trainees, he weaves together their tales of heroism or tragedy with Canada's early aviation history and First World War aviators."

MATHIAS JOOST retired from the Directorate of History, Department of National Defence

IN OUR YOUTH

The Lives, Adventures, and Sacrifices of Early Canadian Flyers

IN OUR YOUTH

Angus Scully

**ANGUS
SCULLY**

Heritage House Publishing Company Ltd.
heritagehouse.ca

Cataloguing information available from Library and Archives Canada
978-1-77203-421-9 (paperback)
978-1-77203-422-6 (e-book)

Edited by Warren Layberry
Proofread by David Marsh
Cover and interior book design by Setareh Ashrafologhalai
Front cover photograph courtesy of Doreen Gagnier O'Keefe
Maps by Eric Leinberger

The interior of this book was produced on FSC®-certified, acid-free
paper, processed chlorine free, and printed with vegetable-based inks.

Heritage House gratefully acknowledges that the land on which
we live and work is within the traditional territories of the Lkwungen
(Esquimalt and Songhees), Malahat, Pacheedaht, Scia'new, T'Sou-ke,
and W̱SÁNEĆ (Pauquachin, Tsartlip, Tsawout, Tseycum) Peoples.

We acknowledge the financial support of the Government of
Canada through the Canada Book Fund (CBF) and the Canada Council
for the Arts, and the Province of British Columbia through the
British Columbia Arts Council and the Book Publishing Tax Credit.

26 25 24 23 22   1 2 3 4 5
Printed in Canada

CONTENTS

INTRODUCTION

INVITE YOU TO join me in a search for the story behind three old pictures of Canadian aviators from the First World War. The search takes us on a journey to a time when flying was brand new and excited the imagination of the world. The story of flight will unfold, and the impact of the war on the lives of Canadians will be uncovered again, but in a different form from the usual war history. The focus of the search is on the young men in the pictures—the youth of Canada in its youth.

We know the names of the young men. Looking into the records of the past has revealed that a few had once been famous, but glory is fleeting. Most are unknown in the history books through no fault of their own—or even of history itself. Time has pushed their stories away, but they are still waiting for rediscovery or revelation.

In finding the stories of these men, we will also find the history of early aviation in Canada—before, during, and after the Great War. Their stories are important because they go beyond the tales (and controversies) about the great aces. Those warriors of the sky, compared to knights of old, have received, and still attract, great attention in books, movies, and countless social media interest groups. The thirty-two young men in the pictures are just as important.

Libraries, archives, and antique stores are full of photos of men from the First World War. There are photos of tens, hundreds, even thousands of men standing in army-smart formations. There are usually no names and sometimes not even the names of the unit. There are also those studio shots of stiffly posed youngsters in new uniforms, now all gone and sadly unknown. In some homes, luckily for the families and for us, there are photos with names. But many just show more of the nameless. Fortunately, the names of all thirty-two men explored in the three main pictures of this book are known, and from that unfolds a story of wonder, daring, bravery, poetry, art, and technology. These three pictures—and all the other photos in this book—are as important in telling the story as are the documents, letters, and histories. View them carefully and you will be looking deep into the past and meeting amazing people. The thirty-two youth in these pictures are us.

This book is not a traditional description of one thing after another. The organization is based on the chronology in which the pictures were made but there is some jumping around in time and place, some digressions, some asides, and some overlap. Repetition is present, and hopefully helps the reader. But, by and by, the reader will know some young men rather well, will have met if only briefly some of the great names, and will have experienced the fascination with flying that gripped the country from 1903 to 1940 and on to the present.

Part One, "Youth Ascending," examines the young men in a photo taken in Toronto in July 1916 at the privately run Curtiss Flying School. They are very young. The stories behind the photo reveal that some are university graduates, one has left McGill University after three years to learn to fly, another is the son of a prominent west coast doctor and politician, another is the younger brother of the man who will command the Canadian First Army in 1944–45, another is a moody, troubled youth. One is too tall. One is thrown out of the Royal Navy's pilot training program because he is not a gentleman. They are among the earliest flyers in Canada. This part also introduces and follows the theme of the mental injury of flying stress, a condition little understood at the time but one with obvious impact on these young Canadians. Who were they and what happened to them?

Part Two, "Youth Lost," begins with a miniature painting—a portrait worn in a locket, every day, by the mother of a young pilot from British Columbia. He is Osborne Orr, a young man largely lost to history until 2019. He has been claimed for years by Americans as an American ace flying with the Royal Flying Corps. He was an ace, but never an American. The story behind this rare colour picture of a First World War aviator reveals a story of rise and fall, of romance and tragedy, of loss, sorrow, and remembrance. Rediscovering Osborne Orr is also the story of how his family found, or perhaps rediscovered, long-obscured items related to Osborne's story. The finding of his long-missing medals, especially the Distinguished Flying Cross, in early 2020 is a wonder. Osborne Orr was perhaps lost, or misplaced, for many decades, but he was in fact quietly remembered every year by his high school in Vancouver. This is also a story about two women who were left in sorrow, and what happened to them.

Part Three, "Youth Transcended," examines two young men who made a major contribution to the early days of civilian flying after 1918. Before becoming flyers, both were sergeants in the army, coming from rather ordinary backgrounds. One, Earl Godfrey, became a member of the Aviation Hall of Fame. Here, however, more attention is paid to George Trim who emerges from the shadows to be revealed as a significant player in the heady days of flying on the west coast in 1919 and 1920. Newly returned to Vancouver in 1919, Trim meets a movie star and royalty, races his plane against cars and trains, performs stunts, crashes spectacularly, and flies deep into the mountains of BC. In 1920, Trim co-founds the first airline company in BC, experiences disappointment, even disgrace, but then a few years later rises again to play a role in the early days of the Royal Canadian Air Force. In Quebec, in the late 1920s, he becomes a respected aviation safety expert and, in 1939 and 1940, plays a significant role in one of the most infamous air tragedies of the time. Flying in 1919 and 1920 was something of a youthful party, and the struggle to bring safety and order to civilian flying is also a theme of this section.

Although character is not ever fully revealed by written records and photos, a sense of character does begin to emerge for many of the thirty-two men in the pictures. We can start to comprehend character from a few words in a confidential report, the importance of the meaning of "keen," a letter home, a photo of a family man, the transcript of a coroner's inquest, a radio broadcast, or the sad hope of parents revealed in a news clipping.

Two artists—one a painter, the other a poet—play a role in helping to understand the feelings of the moment. These artists are not the subjects of the photos, but they are related. They were on the scene, just out of view beyond the edges of the pictures, people who knew several of our young men. What the artists tried to portray is important to our stories.

If the sensibilities of artists play a role in the stories, so too does modern digital technology, which has forced a revolution in research. Most of the young men are unknown, not because they accomplished nothing, but because their records, their lives, are buried in paper. The digital revolution has made it possible to "unearth" them.

So, join me in looking behind the pictures and discover some remarkable young Canadians and the story of early flying in Canada.

1

YOUTH
ASCENDING

A SCARCE-REMEMBERED
DREAM

And yet they were little more than children,
these mere boys who had brought the
lustre of everlasting fame to the British aviation
service. Some are scarce eighteen. It is
rare to find a flying man over twenty-five.

WILLIAM AVERY BISHOP
Winged Warfare[1]

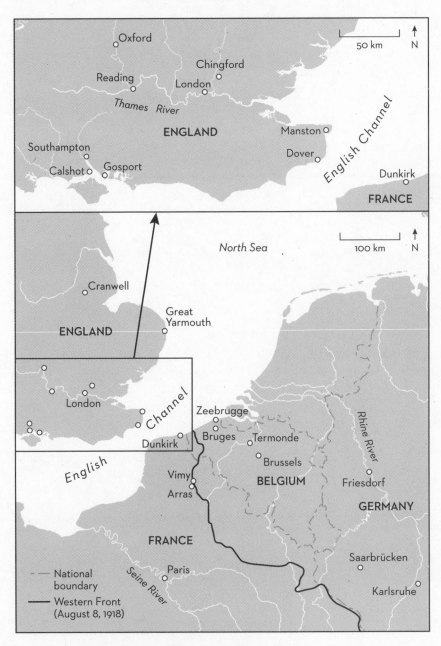

Western Europe during the First World War.

YOUNG MEN LOOK back at us from July 1916, posed in front of an airplane. They look like comrades, relaxed with each other. It was summer, and some of them had been playing baseball when Lemuel Blakemore, the photographer, came and set up his camera. Blakemore was originally from Minneapolis but had operated businesses in Minnesota then in Winnipeg and had been in business in Toronto for only a few months when he took this picture.[2] In many old photos, people have a stiff, posed look. Here they look quite "modern." It could be the casual clothes or their casual stance. They could be boys we know. Look carefully and you could swear you know one of them at least. Blakemore did a wonderful job of capturing their youth.

These young men are the students, instructors, and mechanics of the Curtiss Flying School, also called the Curtiss School of Aviation. The school was at Long Branch, in what is now the western part of the city of Toronto.

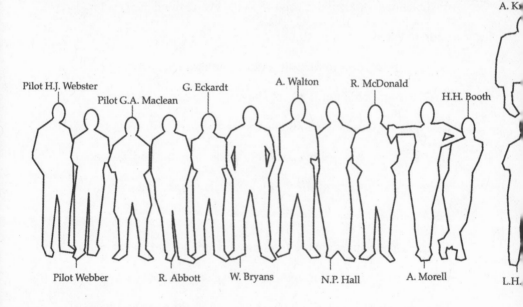

Pilot H.J. Webster

Pilot G.A. Maclean

G. Eckardt

A. Walton

R. McDonald

H.H. Booth

A. Ki

Pilot Webber

R. Abbott

W. Bryans

N.P. Hall

A. Morell

L.H.

TOP Curtiss Flying School, class of July 1916, Toronto. COURTESY OF TORONTO
PUBLIC LIBRARY X23-4 CAB.III

BOTTOM ILLUSTRATION COURTESY OF WARREN LAYBERRY

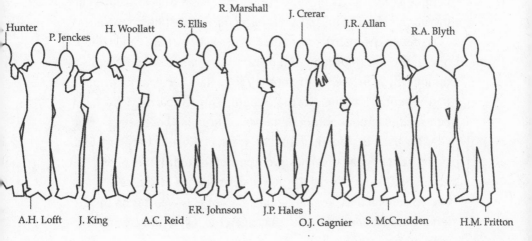

Hunter   P. Jenckes   H. Woollatt   S. Ellis   R. Marshall   J. Crerar   J.R. Allan   R.A. Blyth

A.H. Lofft   J. King   A.C. Reid   F.R. Johnson   J.P. Hales   O.J. Gagnier   S. McCrudden   H.M. Fritton

While they stood there in the hot Toronto summer sun, the battle of the Somme raged in France, a battle killing and wounding tens of thousands of other young men. They were far from the danger of war, but they were not planning to avoid war, indeed they were planning to become involved in one of the deadliest parts of that far-off World War. They were taking flying lessons so that they could join the Royal Naval Air Service or the Royal Flying Corps, in England. Behind them is one of the training aircraft operated by the Curtiss School. It is a JN-3, designed by Glenn Curtiss in the United States and built by the Curtiss Aeroplane and Motor Company in Toronto. Both the factory and the school were managed by Canada's most famous flyer, Douglas McCurdy.

Can you spot the youngest of them? Count six from the right and there is J. Crerar. His full name was Malcolm Charlton Crerar, born 11 July 1897. He had just turned eighteen. He is not the only one with a misspelling or incorrect initial in his name, but it is definitely him according to the written records and other photos. There are four aged nineteen: R. Abbott, N. Hall, A. Morrell, and A. Walton. Of the twenty-three students, five were teenagers. Can you spot the man who became a very good pilot but, at six foot five, was too big to fit into fighting aircraft and, in England, was assigned to instruction in seaplanes?

Three of the instructors at the Curtiss School, here called pilots, are on the left. Missing is American Bert Acosta, who became a famous flyer in the 1920s and 1930s. Another American pilot had recently left the Curtiss School, Guy Gilpatric, who later became the famous author of the *Mr. Glencannon* book series. Pilot G.A. Maclean is older, in flying terms quite old, at twenty-five. His riding pants, called breeches, were part of the uniform of pilots. He had already served in the Royal Naval Air Service in France but had been discharged as a result of illness. Pilot H.J. Webster on the far left looks a bit of a rogue with that cigarette holder and the grin. He remains a mystery.

Pilot Thomas William Webber is the oldest man in the photo, at age thirty. He had graduated from the Curtiss Flying School the previous summer and served briefly in England with the Royal Naval Air Service. His story, to be told later, is one of determination and tragedy.

It is now well over a hundred years since this photo was taken. Can we find the stories behind the picture at this late date? It is fortunate that their names are included, for there are thousands of photos of military units, with thousands of anonymous young men in them, and now there is no way of knowing who they were, never mind of telling their stories. So, the names help a lot, but there are no truly famous men among them whose life stories were written closer to the time. There are no diaries, no boxes of letters, no later scholarly inquiries into the character of a man who became a great hero in the war or a prominent citizen in the years following the war. They were ordinary, yet very special at the same time because they were aviators. However, in the digital age it is possible to mine the data—the military records now online, or the newspapers, digitized and searchable. As has always been the case, archives and libraries can be searched, but the digital revolution has made access much easier and cheaper. We can recreate some of their story and, with luck, make connections.

For these youthful flyers, the records of the Curtiss Flying School are preserved in the Library and Archives Canada in Ottawa. When they passed their tests, they were registered with the Royal Aero Club in London, England, usually with a photo. These records are now digitized and searchable. Once the men were in the service, more complete records were kept, and in the case of the Royal Naval Air Service, with more candour than in the Royal Flying Corps. From these records it is possible to tell part of the story behind this picture. Consider the following before the history behind the picture unfolds:

1. There are twenty-nine young men in the photo, three of whom are mechanics.

2. There are also three men identified as pilots on the left. These are the instructors.

3. Seventeen of the students served overseas in the Royal Naval Air Service, two in the Royal Flying Corps. Two of the instructors had already served overseas.

4. Altogether they shot down over twenty-five enemy aircraft.

5. Seven received awards for "gallantry in the face of the enemy." Two were awarded the Distinguished Service Cross, and five were mentioned in dispatches.

6. Three became aces.

7. Four were court-martialled for breaking military law.

8. Four had physical wounds, one losing his left arm.

9. At least four suffered a psychological disorder, then called neurasthenia, emotional shock, or flying sickness. Whatever the term, today we recognize these psychological disorders as wounds caused by the stress of combat flying.[3]

10. Three were later discharged from the service as medically unfit, two suffering from stomach ulcers.

11. Two were shot down behind enemy lines and became prisoners of war in Germany.

12. Six were killed.

Canada's Aviation Pioneers

There were so few pilots in Canada in 1916 that all these young men can be considered aviation pioneers. But without Alexander Graham Bell, there would not have been a Curtiss Flying School in Toronto or perhaps even any Canadian aviation at all. How could the inventor of the telephone be so important in Canadian aviation?

Born in Scotland, Bell lived briefly in Brantford, Ontario, then moved to the United States where he patented the telephone and started the Bell Telephone Company. Importantly for Canada, he had a summer home called Beinn Bhreagh at Baddeck in Cape Breton, Nova Scotia, and spent the entire summer there every year.

At this summer home, Bell conducted experiments in many fields of science and invited experts to join him. He also employed local people to help, including J.A. Douglas McCurdy, who was also a student in engineering at the University of Toronto.

Bell was interested in movement through water and air. He experimented with kites, gliders, propellers, and wings. After McCurdy graduated as a mechanical engineer, Bell hired him and another young University of Toronto engineer, Frederick Walker "Casey" Baldwin, to work with him on his experiments. Bell also invited to Baddeck a young American manufacturer of lightweight engines and motorcycles, Glenn Curtiss. The last member of this youthful team was US Army Lieutenant Thomas Selfridge. At the suggestion of Bell's wife, and with her financial backing, they formed the Aerial Experiment Association in 1907. In winter, when the Bell family was not in Cape Breton, the team worked from Hammondsport, New York, near the Curtiss factory.[4] The first powered aircraft of the AEA was designed by Thomas Selfridge and was called Red Wing. Away on business, Selfridge was unable to be pilot of his own machine on its first flight. Glenn Curtiss described that flight at Keuka Lake, New York, on 12 March 1908.

From left: "Casey" Baldwin, Tom Selfridge, Glenn Curtiss, Alexander Graham Bell, J.A.D. McCurdy of the Aerial Experiment Association, and Augustus Post, a famous early aviator acting as an observer for the Aero Club of America. In the Bell family, they were called "the youngsters." MAJOR JAMES MATTHEWS COLLECTION, CITY OF VANCOUVER ARCHIVES. AM54-S4-2-: CVA 371-2326

Baldwin climbed into the seat, took the control in hand and we cranked the motor. When we released our hold of the machine, it sped over the ice like a scared rabbit for two or three hundred feet, and then much to our joy, it jumped into the air. Rising to a height of six or eight feet, Baldwin flew the unheard-of distance of three hundred and eighteen feet, eleven inches. We had achieved the first public flight of a heavier than air machine in America.[5]

"Casey" Baldwin was the first Canadian to fly. Orville and Wilbur Wright had made the first-ever powered flight in a heavier than air flying machine in 1903, but they were very secretive about their operations and had not made a public flight. Only after the AEA made public flights did the Wrights do so. Thomas Selfridge, although working with the rival AEA, was, as an army officer, able to visit the Wrights' operations. He was killed while flying as a passenger with Orville Wright in September 1908. Selfridge was the first person in history to die in an aircraft accident.

In 1920, McCurdy recalled his role and the accomplishments of the AEA.

In the summer of 1907 there was formed at Baddeck, Nova Scotia, the Aerial Experiment Association. The members of this association were Dr. Bell, F.W. Baldwin, Lieutenant Thomas Selfridge, U.S.A., Glenn H. Curtiss and myself. The association conducted experiments during the summer and fall of 1907 at Baddeck with tetrahedral kites, with motors and with serial propellers mounted on boats. In December 1907, it was decided to move to Hammondsport, New York, where Mr. Curtiss had a factory and to there build a glider. This move was made on December 24th. We proceeded at Hammondsport to experiment with gliders and then to build machines which would fly, the members of the association working together, although each one in turn had general charge of the design of a machine. The first machine made was called "Red Wing" and on March 12, 1908, flew for 318 feet and 11 inches. Following the construction of the "Red Wing", other machines were made, one called the "Silver Dart", being designed by me, and in this machine I made a flight on December 12, 1908. These were the first public flights which had ever been made in aeroplanes. I subsequently took the "Silver Dart" to Nova Scotia and continued flying it through the winter in 1909, making many flights and covering in all, more than one thousand miles. The flights which I made with the "Silver Dart" in Canada were the first flights which had ever been made in the British Empire. The Aerial Experiment Association continued throughout part of 1909 and as a result of our experiments, there developed the system of control through ailerons. This system of control through ailerons was so extensively used by Mr. Curtiss and was such an important feature of the Curtiss machines that it was known as the Curtiss control.[6]

The AEA disbanded in 1910, but Bell, McCurdy, and Baldwin formed the Canadian Aerodrome Company and tried to interest the Canadian military in flying.[7] McCurdy and Baldwin took the Silver Dart and the Baddeck—another of their designs—to Ottawa. Colonel G.S. Maunsell, Chief of Engineering Services at the Ministry of Militia and Defence, was impressed and wrote a series of reports for the minister, Sir Sam Hughes; however, Hughes rejected all proposals, not seeing any role for aviation.[8]

Baldwin continued to work with Bell. In 1919, he set a world water-speed record in a hydrofoil boat that he and Bell designed. That year, Bell also hired Baldwin to be the manager of his Cape Breton estate, Beinn Bhreagh, and its labs.

McCurdy continued to work with Curtiss, who is now recognized not just as a pioneer flyer but also as a great designer and manufacturer of aircraft. McCurdy described what they accomplished.

In 1909 the Curtiss Exhibition Company was formed and I took part in the work of this Company. For several years I gave exhibition flights in practically every state of the United States east of the Mississippi River and also in Mexico. The purpose of these exhibitions was to advertise Curtiss machines and to obtain funds with which to carry on the further development of the aeroplane. In 1909, I conducted the first wireless experiments at Sheepshead Bay Race Track in conjunction with the New York World and for the first time sent from an aeroplane a wireless message. After the

McCurdy's historic flight in the Silver Dart was nicely Canadian. It took off from and landed on the ice of Bras d'Or Lake with attendants on skates.

CANADA AVIATION AND SPACE MUSEUM ARCHIVES; 15495

first of January, 1910, I carried on these experiments in Florida and succeeded in both sending and receiving messages. In 1910, I made the first flight across water out of sight of land flying from Key West, Florida to Havana, Cuba, a distance of one hundred and ten miles. During this time I frequently carried messages and passengers for the purpose of demonstrating the uses to which the aeroplane could be put.[9]

McCurdy was still working with Curtiss when war broke out.

Canadians Wanted to Fly—and Fight

Although Sir Sam Hughes had rejected aviation in 1910, he did create a short-lived aviation corps for the Canadian Army in 1914. Two men who claimed to know aviation got the attention of Sir Sam and were hired to buy an American aircraft and have it shipped to England. Damaged in transit, the machine never flew, and the Canadian air corps disappeared. The whole affair remains something of a mystery in Canadian aviation history, and in fact seems at times to have been a con. It was very irregular.

McCurdy was the greatest and most experienced Canadian aviator in 1914. In December, he wrote to Prime Minister Robert Borden and again proposed an aviation corps for the army. He offered to build a factory in Toronto to manufacture Curtiss machines. He also offered to train pilots. Borden was not interested, but he did pass the proposal on to British authorities.[10] The lack of interest by the Canadian government is usually explained by both the newness of the technology and the costs. In fairness, the Canadian government was not alone in being confused about what use aircraft might have. Many people were not inspired by the flimsy, crash-prone machines built by the Wright brothers, or Glenn Curtiss, or McCurdy and Baldwin. They seemed more like circus acts.

The British, on the other hand, did create flying services—the Royal Flying Corps for the army and the Royal Naval Air Service. These were small, and their aircraft not much advanced on the Silver Dart or Baddeck. British authorities could see some potential in McCurdy's proposal and made a deal. Ottawa agreed to allow the British to recruit Canadians for the Royal Flying Corps and the Royal Naval Air Service. McCurdy would build a factory in Toronto and a flying school. In February 1915, the Curtiss Aeroplane and Motor Company was incorporated with fifty thousand dollars in capital. McCurdy was the president and managing director in Toronto. The flying school was at Long Branch—now in the western part of the city of Toronto, on the shore of Lake Ontario. The aerodrome that McCurdy built there was Canada's first real airport.

The British were interested in getting Canadian pilots, but those young men would have to bear some of the burden of the cost of their training. Prospective recruits had to be between nineteen and thirty years of age, and there were unspoken social requirements. As historian S.F. Wise put it, those requirements and the high fees "restricted entry, in the main, to young men from families more comfortably situated than the generality of Canadians."[11] If they passed a medical and an interview with British officers in Ottawa, they would be admitted to the Curtiss Flying School in Toronto and have to pay tuition of four hundred dollars. Only if they graduated with four hundred minutes of flying time and were granted a certificate from the Royal Aero Club would the British then refund their tuition—or most of it.

Young men could seek acceptance by either the Royal Naval Air Service or the Royal Flying Corps. In 1915, neither wanted large numbers of flyers, and there could be quite a waiting period. They might also seek training at a private American school. Another alternative was to join the army and, once overseas in Britain or France, ask to transfer to one of the flying services. In Canada, the RNAS was, at first, the more preferred service. It paid more and offered the recruits an immediate officer's commission in the Royal Navy once they had graduated from the Curtiss school. The RFC accepted them merely as cadets, a lower rank at lower pay. In the war, 807 Canadians served in the RNAS and 279 were killed. It has been estimated that ten percent of the officers of the RNAS were Canadians.[12]

The two-seat Curtiss JN-3 training plane was a stable platform though the engine was a bit underpowered. With the student in the front seat, the instructor shouted instructions from the rear—or tried to, over the engine and wind noise. There were dual controls. Around and around in the sky over Long Branch, the school's four planes were up and flying when the weather permitted, and when there were no breakdowns. With delays and taking turns, there was a lot of waiting. And baseball. There was little ground instruction on the theory of flying.

The final exam required three solo flights, two involving a figure eight around two posts that were 500 yards (457 metres) apart.

There was no looping or spinning. Gentle banks were about the limit of the manoeuvres. On the third test flight, students had to gain one hundred metres in altitude, then cut the motor and glide to a landing. There were no brakes on early aircraft, and the pilots had to coast to within fifty metres of a designated spot.[13] In 1915, some students were also taught to fly seaplanes from a Curtiss school on Toronto Island.

At the end of July 1915, the first flyers graduated from Toronto—eight for the RNAS and three for the RFC. Training continued slowly over the summer. Among the grads were Claire MacLaurin, who would within five years be playing a major role in the development of aviation in Canada, and Thomas William Webber, the "Pilot Webber" of our picture. How he ended up back in Toronto a year later tells us a lot about social attitudes at the time.

McCurdy probably took more interest in the building of aircraft. The JN-3 engines were built by a Curtiss plant in nearby Buffalo, New York. The Toronto plant built the airframes and installed the engines. Most of the completed machines went to the British, with a few planes reserved for the Curtiss School to replace damaged machines. These early flying machines were easily damaged. Accidents were frequent.

McCurdy Weathers a Scandal

In November 1915, the Curtiss Flying School closed for the winter. McCurdy clearly had some experience with winter flying, but he was not prepared to continue the school's operations in a snowy Toronto winter on the shore of Lake Ontario. This decision left 250 young men stranded, either unable to complete the training they had started, or stranded on the waiting list. McCurdy promised refunds, but the young men were anxious to fly and wanted to be able to go ahead. They approached Sam Hughes for help, but he advised them to join the army. The newspapers cried fraud, calling the Curtiss Flying School a bunco scheme. The story made the news across Canada. The *Calgary Herald* reported on 6 November.

AVIATION STUDENTS HAVE BEEN BUNCOED
Likely to be Trouble for Promoters of Curtiss School Toronto

In an effort to secure better treatment from the government and Curtiss school of aviation, a meeting of students was held at Toronto Canoe Club yesterday. In spite of the repeated assurances by A.F. Barr, secretary of the Curtiss aviation institutions, that all the students would receive a refund of $375 of the $400 fee, the students have received word from Col. Staunton... Representative in Canada of the Royal Flying Corps, that he had little hope the war office would refund any portion to any student who had not qualified for his pilot's license. This puts many of the students in a very embarrassing position, as in a number of cases, the money was borrowed on the strength of Mr. Barr's promise.[14]

In the end, the students were not "buncoed." Candidates for both the RFC and the RNAS eventually made it to England to complete their training.[15]

The Curtiss Flying School, Toronto, 1916

With the arrival of spring 1916, a new flying season started at Long Branch. There were new instructors and a private foundation offering to pay for increased flight time for the students. The Canadian Aviation Fund, based on private donations to the British government, paid for increased time beyond the basic 400 minutes needed for the Royal Aero Club Certificate. Of the sixty-three grads in the 1916 season, three-quarters took advantage and got 480 or more minutes. In fact, thirteen got 600 minutes, and three

Pilot Bert Acosta (left), Chief Engineer Ericson of Canadian Aeroplanes Ltd. (centre), and Pilot Webster (right) in 1915. The pilots were about to test the first Curtiss JN-4 Canuck. Webster is the tall character on the left in the group photo from 1916. Although little is known about him, he instructed young pilots for two flying seasons in Toronto. CANADA DEPARTMENT OF NATIONAL DEFENCE/LIBRARY AND ARCHIVES CANADA. PA-025174

got 720.[16] The school might produce better pilots, but the increased time limited the output of grads. Still, it was hoped that improved basic training would produce better service pilots.

Aviation was so new that one of the first challenges McCurdy faced in 1915, and again in 1916, was finding instructors. In 1914, there had been only eight certified pilots in Canada. Those available were, by the nature of flying, themselves youths. One of the pilots hired by McCurdy in 1915 was twenty-year-old Bert Acosta from the Curtiss operations in California. He taught flying in Toronto during the 1915 and 1916 flying seasons. When the US entered the war in 1917, Acosta became the chief instructor of the Aviation Section of the US Signal Corps, then the American version of an air force. He went on to have a distinguished and at times controversial career in aviation.

Two of the instructors hired for the 1916 season were graduates from the 1915 class of the Curtiss Flying School. Royal Navy records state Thomas Webber was a married man, born in 1886 and living at 306 Harbord Street in Toronto. He passed from the Curtiss Flying School on 9 September 1915 and was issued Royal Aero Club Certificate No. 1854.[17] The photo accompanying his registration in the RAC shows him looking quite smart in naval uniform—a probationary flight sub-lieutenant of the Royal Navy. His family and friends must have been proud of this accomplishment. He was off for advanced flight training, clearly eager to serve King and country.

A Shocking Turn of Events

Pilot Webber was dismissed from the Royal Navy in December 1915. A transcript of his record speaks volumes.

> I do not consider that this officer is at all suitable to hold a commission in H.M. Service. He is quite unfit socially and unable to talk or write English correctly. He fails in conversation to aspirate his H's and constructs his sentences ungrammatically. He does not appear to have previously associated with gentlemen on terms of equality. I regret that I cannot give a very impartial opinion on his value as a pilot. Owing to constant bad weather and lack of sound machines, I have not had much opportunity of watching him fly. He has, however, made four flights on Curtiss machines, on two of which he damaged the machine when landing.
>
> I consider his general behaviour brings discredit upon the service, as he cannot understand that officers in uniform do not behave like the people he has previously associated with. I have

	CURTISS AEROPLANES & MOTORS, LIMITED. AVIATION SCHOOL. Daily Flying Record For Week Ending July 25 1916. Pilot _Webber_											
No.	NAME	TOTAL TO DATE	WED. 19	THU. 20	FRI. 21	SAT. 22	SUN. 23	MON. 24	TUE. 25	TOTAL FOR WEEK	TOTAL LAST WEEK	TOTAL TO DATE
	Midshall				17 17	12 12	10 10			39		39
	Titton			7 7	16 20	36				43		43
	Hales			21 21	11 18	29				50		50
	Shaw				12 12	13 37				37		37
	Eckhardt			11 11	14 10	24				35		35
	Whitfield			11 11	21 21	17 17				49		49
	Davis			10 10	12 12	16 16				38		38
	Bryans			11 11	15 15	13 13				39		39
	Scott				12 12	20 20	16 16			48		48
	Burt				11 11	11 11	18 18			40		40
	Tests TOTALS		147			9 9				156		156
	Totals		147	71	40	226	90			574		574

OPPOSITE This is the Royal Aero Club registration photo of Probationary Flight Sub-lieutenant Webber. He had volunteered to fight and was keen to fly.
ROYAL AERO CLUB AVIATOR'S CERTIFICATES, ALBUM 5. COURTESY ROYAL AERO CLUB TRUST

ABOVE The logbook of Webber's first week as an instructor. Students were assigned to the same instructor each week until they graduated. LIBRARY AND ARCHIVES CANADA. DAILY FLYING RECORDS, JULY 1916. CURTISS SCHOOL OF AVIATION FONDS, MG28 III 65 VOL 1

never been able to entrust any duties to him and he has proved quite useless in every way.[18]

It was not enough to have failed as a flyer. Webber was dismissed from the Royal Navy in March 1916 and returned to Canada. Today, over a century later in a different social era, it is difficult to fully fathom what happened to this man.

Whatever his shortcomings in the Royal Navy, Webber seems to have been a successful instructor at the Curtiss School.

Determined to Fight, Determined to Fly

The other named instructor in the photo about whom there are records is Gerald Arthur Maclean. He was born in Toronto in 1891 and lived at 82 Highland Avenue in the wealthy neighbourhood of Rosedale. He joined the army in 1915 at the age of twenty-three and became a lieutenant in the Eaton Machine Gun Battery. His attestation papers say he was single, occupation lumberman. He sailed to England with his unit in June 1915.[19]

Sir John Craig Eaton was the head of the T. Eaton Company, one of the largest department stores in North America. Founded by Timothy Eaton in 1869 in Toronto, Eaton's stores and its catalogue shopping dominated retail sales in Canada. Sir John Eaton encouraged his employees to enlist, paying married men their regular Eaton's salary on top of their military pay, and paying single men half of their Eaton's salary. In addition, all goods supplied by Eaton's for the Canadian war effort were provided at cost. Sir John donated a hundred thousand dollars to raise the Eaton Machine Gun Battery and purchase "quick firing machine guns mounted on armoured trucks."[20] Eaton's donation bought fifteen, and the government bought twenty-five more. Maclean appears not to have been an employee of Eaton's, but the Eaton Machine Gun Battery was a prestigious outfit and it specifically recruited athletes.

Flight Sub-lieutenant Gerald Arthur Maclean. This is the photo he submitted to the Royal Aero Club. He was soon flying seaplanes over the English Channel and German-occupied Belgium. ROYAL AERO CLUB AVIATOR'S CERTIFICATES, ALBUM 5. COURTESY ROYAL AERO CLUB TRUST

Curtiss Aeroplanes & Motors, Limited. Aviation School

Daily Flying Record For Week Ending _Aug 8_ 19_16_   Pilot _Maclean_

No.	Name	Total to Date	WED 2	THU 3	FRI 4	SAT 5	SUN 6	MON 7	TUE 8	Total for Week	Total Last Week	Total to Date
	Smith	331	20			18				38	11	369
	Major	303				5				0		303
	Hall	355	14					14		28		383
✓	Gagnier	386			24			18		42		428
	Jencks	250	20	8				13		41		291
	Abbott	339	10	5	2			16		33	36	372
	Cruzner	294	18			15		16		49	6	343
✓	Steele	322				18		12		30	19	352
✓	McDonald	345								0	18	345
	Creear	281	12			14				26	3	307
	Totals	736	7		9 13	15 15				35	19	171
	Totals	3352	101	13	39	80		89		322	22	3674

Maclean's logbook from the Curtiss Flying School for 8 August 1916 shows how slow student progress could be. Student Gagnier reached the 400-minute mark in training, but others accumulated very little. Students had to wait for the turns of others, weather, maintenance, and fueling. If a machine's motor needed replacing, a not uncommon event, pilot and students might wait for a whole week. LIBRARY AND ARCHIVES CANADA. DAILY FLYING RECORDS, AUG.–SEPT. 1916. CURTISS SCHOOL OF AVIATION FONDS, MG28 III 65 VOL 1

Only a few months after going overseas, Lieutenant Maclean applied to transfer to the RNAS, was accepted, and began flight training in England in October 1915. The records show no reason for the transfer, but it may have been that he "fell for flying." He passed his RAC certificate on 17 November 1915. After advanced training, he was posted on 1 January 1916, to HMS *Riviera*, a seaplane carrier that was part of the famous Dover Patrol. The ship operated in the English Channel and provided a mobile base for the seaplanes, lifting them into and out of the water with a crane. The seaplanes were used for aerial reconnaissance and bombing. His commanding officer on the ship wrote that Maclean was "a zealous young officer. Has good bearing."

Royal Navy records show that Maclean became ill with albuminuria, a kidney disease, in March 1916. He was declared unfit for further service, his commission was terminated, and he was returned to Canada. He may have been too ill to serve, but he was clearly determined to play a role in the war effort as an instructor.

Maclean did not give up. When the Curtiss Flying School in Toronto was taken over by the Royal Flying Corps in January 1917, Maclean asked to be reinstated in the RNAS. He was denied, on medical grounds. Yet again, he persisted and applied to the Royal Flying Corps. The RFC was very short of pilots and accepted Maclean. His new records begin with him in England, assigned to the 110 Squadron. Then, yet again, his health problems appeared. In September 1918 when 110 Squadron went to France, Maclean was promoted to temporary Captain but transferred to No. 5 Training Depot Station as a Flight Commander, Ground Duties. When the war ended, he remained on duty until January 1919, when he was declared "permanently unfit for further service in the Royal Air Force. Army Category F." In February 1919, the records state, "relinquished commission on account of ill health and permitted to retain rank." [21]

Gerald Maclean wanted to fly and to fight, but ill health kept him out of combat flying. He was a good instructor. He lived until 1965.

The Mechanics

Successful flying is based on many factors, including good maintenance and supply. Early aircraft, and the Curtiss JN-3 was one of the first, were fragile and early aircraft motors were unreliable without constant maintenance. Mechanics were fundamental to any flying program, and their presence in the photo suggests that this was understood and appreciated. They are part of the group. These technical personnel are too often left out of the story.[22]

Mechanic L.H. Briggs does not appear in the records of the army, the RFC, the RNAS, or the RAF. After 1916, he may have kept on being a mechanic in the Toronto factory. During the war, there was a real shortage of mechanics in both the services and the civilian world, and many of them stayed in the civilian market where they could earn more. There are military officer's records for an E.A. Hunter and a J.B. King. The Royal Air Force record for E.A. Hunter of Edmonton is just a few lines, showing that he became a flying cadet in 1918, a few weeks before the war ended. He was granted an honorary commission when the war ended.[23] J.B. King's equally brief record shows that he was discharged from the RAF in Toronto in December 1918, having just started ground training as a cadet.[24] Neither record proves conclusively that they were the same men named in the Curtiss photo, but it is of course possible that, after years of repairing aircraft, they decided in 1918 that they wanted to fly and fight. We might speculate that the RAF would have preferred to employ them as mechanics. Famously, Englishman James McCudden was a mechanic in the RFC in 1914. He became a pilot in 1916, progressed to ace in 1917 and was credited with shooting down fifty-seven enemy aircraft before he was killed in a flying accident in 1918. He was awarded the Victoria Cross. Making the transition from mechanic to pilot was possible, but mechanics were skilled specialists, and there never seemed to be enough of them.

Slow Progress

The logbooks of the Curtiss Aviation School show the slow progress of learning to fly in Toronto and the amount of time spent just waiting for a turn. Each pilot instructor had one machine and ten pupils although, at times, Acosta had more assigned to him. The weekly flying log ran from Wednesday to Tuesday, and flying took place every day, if possible. The week ending 25 July 1916 was one of the best flying weeks of the summer. Acosta's fourteen students spent a combined 577 minutes in the air, with the beginners getting less time as final test flights were run on several days and everyone had to wait. Maclean's ten were out for a total of 906 minutes, with flying cancelled on Thursday morning because of high winds. Webber's ten had 574 total minutes with two days lost to motor trouble. Webster's ten had 537 minutes aloft, again with time lost for motor trouble and a "broken tail."[25]

Motor troubles and weather cost the students a lot of time. In June, Webster's students had to wait four days for a new motor to be installed. Although Maclean's pupils got the most time in the air the week ending July 26, the very next week they lost five days waiting for a new motor, and then when it was installed, student Abbott made the first flight but broke "the landing chassis," and everyone else lost another day. Webber's students in the first week of August lost the whole week. His log records "new machine and motor." The logs also show that a storm hit during the week ending 20 June, and the whole school was grounded for four days. Even when flying was not interrupted, a student might on some days get as few as ten minutes in the air. The later service records of some of the young men show that they were energetic and often got into trouble. There was plenty of time for more than baseball.

Taking Flight—Two Who Started Together

The pace may have been slow, but students did pass and go overseas. Oliver Joseph Gagnier completed his 400 minutes on 8 August 1916 (see the image on page 30). He was registered with the Royal Aero Club on 15 August. Three days later, Arthur McBurney Walton was registered with the RAC. Walton is on the left in the photo, Gagnier near the right end. They did not take up the offer of the Canadian Aviation Fund to get more minutes of flying time.

Then things happened quickly. First, they went to Ottawa and the Royal Navy offices there and received their officer's commission as probationary flight sub-lieutenants. Then they crossed the Atlantic under military orders. The Royal Navy records show that Gagnier and Walton entered training at the Crystal Palace induction centre in London, England, on 17 September. The Crystal Palace was a huge exhibition centre built in the 1850s and famous around the world at the time. Marching, saluting, and dressing properly were learned along with how to fire a revolver, rifle, and the Lewis machine gun. There were also lectures on aero engines and the theory of flight.[26] On 14 October, Gagnier and Walton completed training at Crystal Palace and entered flight training at Cranwell, England.

Cranwell may have been the largest aerodrome in Britain at the time. There were hundreds of aircraft of various types, including some scouts such as the Sopwith Pup and the Nieuport, for advanced flying training. John Playford Hales, another of the young men in the photo, commented on the changes the Curtiss grads faced.

"When I think of the slow old Curtiss it tickles me to think of the surprise the pilots of them will get when they climb in a regular bus and she takes their breath away. Fancy what they will think when they go straight down for 12 000 feet."[27]

By 1917, the Curtiss planes in Canada were doing things in the air that might have surprised Hales. The war changed training—as will be seen in Parts Two and Three.

To "pass out" of Cranwell, there were flying tests and written examinations in meteorology, navigation, theory of flight, engines, armament, and signals. Gagnier and Walton graduated and were assigned to Naval 6 Squadron in France.

Oliver Joseph Gagnier

On 14 January 1917, Oliver Joseph Gagnier was rated as a very good pilot and a "keen and good officer" in his confidential report from Cranwell.[28] On 18 January his record states, "Graduated a Pilot, Recommended for Scouts, Foreign Service." Scouts was the term for fighter planes. On 25 February 1917, he was with Naval 6 Squadron in Dunkirk, flying Nieuport scouts.[29]

Oliver Joseph Gagnier came from an old French-Canadian family but was born in Michigan, in 1896, while his mother was visiting her sister there.[30] He grew up in Toronto, attending De La Salle College for his high school education. He loved the outdoors—camping, snowshoeing, skiing, hunting, fishing. He also played hockey and tennis and loved the piano. He spoke both English and French. At age fifteen, he was accepted at McGill University in Montreal to study engineering but had to wait until he was sixteen to attend. His family was also in Montreal at this time and enrolled him in a school run by the Christian Brothers until he was old enough for McGill. After three years, he left McGill without completing his degree to enter the Curtiss Flying School in Toronto.[31] He was twenty years old.

When Gagnier arrived at Naval 6 in France in early 1917, he must have been a great asset to a squadron that was struggling to operate its new Nieuport scouts. Gagnier's technical skills were undoubted, but just as important would be the fact that he spoke French.[32] This

OPPOSITE Before he left Toronto, Oliver Gagnier had this studio portrait photo taken for his Royal Aero Club registration, showing him with his RAC pin on his lapel. A fine-looking young man, and an ideal recruit for the RNAS. ROYAL AERO CLUB AVIATOR'S CERTIFICATES, 1910–50. ALBUM 10. COURTESY ROYAL AERO CLUB TRUST

ABOVE Gagnier (right) with the other pilots of A Flight, 6 Naval Squadron RNAS. Gagnier looks confident and capable. DOREEN GAGNIER O'KEEFE, DAUGHTER OF O.J. GAGNIER

would ease relations with the people living near their aerodrome and with French flyers. Throughout the services, the ability to speak French became a valuable skill. So too was piano playing, as singing was an important part of life in the officers' mess. After the war, a common feature of reunions was the singing of the old songs from the war. A piano player could really "make" a party, and parties were a common part of mess life as young men let off steam after days of aerial combat.

Gagnier should have felt comfortable in Naval 6. Arthur Walton from the Curtiss School arrived with him, although there is no record of them being friends. Already there from the 1915 Curtiss

School were Percy Beasley from Victoria, BC, George MacLennan from Eugenia, Ontario, Ron Redpath from Montreal, and George Stevens from Peterborough, Ontario.[33]

Naval 6 Squadron was re-equipping with a new scout, the Nieuport 17bis. These machines were a modification of the Nieuport 17 that had been very successful and were loved by Canadian ace Billy Bishop. But the 17bis was plagued with mechanical problems, and the squadron struggled to become operational—that is, able to take part in combat. There were constant engine failures. The gear that allowed the machine gun to fire through the propeller, an interrupter gear, would break down. The fuel pressure system would fail. To some extent the problem was maintenance and the ability of the squadron's mechanics and other technicians to find and correct problems. The squadron leader could be held responsible for the organization and capabilities of his men to get the squadron airborne. The problems were so severe that, in the midst of the deadly aerial combat of April 1917, known as "Bloody April," when every machine was needed and the RFC and RNAS were suffering unprecedented losses, Naval 6 was moved to a quieter front.

April 1917 is remembered in Canada for the great victory by the Canadian Corps at the battle of Vimy Ridge. In the air, the German air force had the upper hand, and its new Albatros D.III scouts were superior machines. Only with the introduction of the Camel, built by the Sopwith company in Britain, would the RFC and the RNAS regain dominance in the air war. Both British air services were in desperate need of pilots.

Perhaps it is unfair to place blame for the squadron's problems on the squadron leader or the mechanics. There was a basic design flaw in the connection of the lower wings to the fuselage. On Friday April 13, Squadron Leader J.J. Petre took up a Nieuport for a test flight. While diving and firing on a practice ground target, the machine broke apart in mid-air and Petre was killed.[34]

O.J. Gagnier (right) with the pilots, mechanics, and other ground crew of A Flight, Naval 6, RNAS. DOREEN GAGNIER O'KEEFE, DAUGHTER OF O.J. GAGNIER

The Nieuport 17bis was not the only aircraft to have problems. Throughout the war, there was a constant struggle on both sides to develop newer, faster machines with more and more firepower, range, or bomb-carrying ability. Engines became a major roadblock. They had to become more powerful and more reliable and yet remain light enough to permit ease of flight. It was a difficult balance to find while developing such a new technology, and modern readers should remember that it was less than ten years since Bell, Curtiss, McCurdy, and Baldwin had made their experiments. Adapting machinery to the cold temperatures of flight at altitudes of five thousand metres or more was also a major problem. Pilots were equipped with hammers, to bash at jammed or frozen machine guns.[35] Despite the mechanical challenges and being in a "quieter" part of the battle, Naval 6 was still a fighting unit and it took part in the aerial war.

Gagnier began combat patrols in early May, after weeks of training flights. On 10 May, he shot down an enemy Albatros fighter. Gagnier's victory took both skill and luck. The book *A History of No. 6 Squadron* described the event.

> Gagnier dived at an angle and caught the Albatros at 7000 feet. He fired two bursts and saw tracers enter the wings and fuselage around the pilot. He got to within 100 feet and fired another burst into the fuselage. The combat was at 5000 feet by this time and the enemy machine was last seen going down in a spinning nose dive northwest of Fresnoy le Grand.[36]

Gagnier was given credit for this victory. A spinning nose dive was often a death sentence, but the pilot might have pulled out at ground level and escaped.

The next day, 11 May, Gagnier was again in the air. At 12:50 PM, he and seven other pilots took off to intercept a German intruder near Melville. They did not find it. At 5:55 PM he was on another patrol at 17,000 feet (5,180 metres), a cold and dangerous place in a single engine, open cockpit Nieuport scout, with no parachute. The British air services did not issue parachutes to their air crew, believing they might take away their offensive spirit. Only observers in balloons had parachutes.

Later at 7:30 PM, while on patrol again, Gagnier saw four enemy aircraft at approximately 4,000 feet (1,220 metres). Unable to get the attention of the rest of the flight, he dived on one of the enemy machines, but his gun jammed. Later he reported that the German pilot was wearing a white sweater and a black leather helmet.[37] Then the other German fighters came after Gagnier. His

Oliver Gagnier standing in front of his Nieuport 17bis scout. With a top speed of 175 kilometres per hour, this plane had a ceiling of 7,000 metres. One Vickers machine gun was synchronized to fire through the propeller arc. There was also a Lewis machine gun mounted on the top of the top wing. The mascot of A Flight looks content. DOREEN GAGNIER O'KEEFE, DAUGHTER OF O.J. GAGNIER

Compare Oliver Gagnier in this photo and the previous ones. The strain is obvious. Despite a grievous injury that ended his flying career, Gagnier was retained in the RNAS and RAF until after the war. He was indeed a keen officer.

DOREEN GAGNIER O'KEEFE, DAUGHTER OF O.J. GAGNIER

Oliver Gagnier in the early 1920s with his first two children, looking again confident and happy. DOREEN GAGNIER O'KEEFE, DAUGHTER OF O.J. GAGNIER

left arm was shattered by a machine gun bullet. He dove to escape but passed out, regaining consciousness in time to pull out of the dive and crash upside down in no man's land, between the German and British trenches. He got out of his machine and took shelter in a shell hole where he again passed out. After again coming to, Gagnier crawled to the British lines and was rushed to a casualty clearing station. On 28 May, he was taken to London, and his left arm was amputated at the shoulder.[38]

Over the summer of 1917, just a year after waiting out the slow training in Toronto, Gagnier slowly healed in London. He asked to stay in the service, and this was granted, but without flight pay. In November he was granted leave in Canada, and he went home to his family in Montreal. He did not return to Europe during the war. In Canada, he spent more time in hospital in Toronto and was promoted to the rank of lieutenant. In November 1918, he married and was assigned to the RAF assistant provost marshal in New York City. He may have been involved in recruiting. He was finally demobilized from RAF Canada in Toronto in September 1919.[39] In Toronto, Gagnier spent several years in a clerical job and then returned to McGill University and became a chartered accountant, setting up a successful practice in Montreal. He and his wife had four children.

His daughter remembered:

> But he wasn't to be stopped and I remember seeing him play tennis, set up tents, chop wood and light a fire and with one hand he would accompany his brother at the piano for duets. I didn't notice that he only had one arm because there was nothing he could not do. Every day it was my treat to watch him shovel coal to "feed the furnace". He would take me out for a drive to a little airport in Montreal where he would watch the airplanes and buy an ice cream cone for a curious child. His behaviour was, and is, a life lesson for me and that I have passed on to my own children.[40]

In 1941, Oliver Gagnier died from cancer, an early death at age forty-five.

Comrades in Naval 6—Gagnier and Walton

Standing seventh from the left in the Curtiss Flying School photo is nineteen-year-old A. Walton—Arthur McBurney Walton. He looks shy. His height earned him the nickname "Stilts." He was born in New York City to Canadian parents in 1896 and raised in the wealthy Toronto neighbourhood of Rosedale, not far from Gerald Maclean. He attended a prestigious private school, Toronto's Upper Canada College.

Walton is something of an enigma. His education meant that, unlike poor Webber, he was used to being in the company of

In the prime of life, looking strong and capable, as usual. Oliver Gagnier adapted well to the loss of an arm. DOREEN GAGNIER O'KEEFE, DAUGHTER OF O.J. GAGNIER

gentlemen. He was a volunteer for a dangerous vocation, but he seems to have been disliked by many his fellow naval pilots, who suspected him of being a shirker. He was sullen and prone to large mood swings.[41] Perhaps that look in the photo is not shyness. The report in his file from flight training at Cranwell, dated 3 February 1917, stated, "Good Pilot. Moderate as an officer; no idea of discipline."[42] But he was not treated like Webber had been at that stage.

In April, Walton was assigned to Naval 6 and, like Gagnier, should have felt welcome with so many other Canadians, and especially with those who had also gone through the Curtiss experience. But as time went by, he ran into trouble. On 1 July 1917 a new commander, after three weeks of observing the pilots, wrote in Walton's confidential report, "Has no idea of discipline." This was the third squadron leader Walton had served under in Naval 6. By the end of July, he had exhausted the patience of his commander, who wrote that his commission should be terminated "as unworthy of detention in the RNAS." Walton was briefly hospitalized with dyspepsia then sent home in August, officially having resigned.[43] In reality, he had no choice, it was that or being cashiered.

This was an extraordinary situation. Walton had been flying with Naval 6 for months and had been credited with forcing down an enemy aircraft. He was sometimes reported as returning early with engine problems, but mechanical problems were common in the squadron. He crashed once, but so did most pilots. Crashing was part of the business. With his background, he should have known how to behave. The many other Canadians in Naval 6 got along, so it was not just snobbery that produced a negative report. Clearly, he was a difficult character.

There is another possibility. One clue is that recorded treatment for dyspepsia, which is a term used to cover pain and burning in the stomach, sometimes with bloody vomit. Among the risk factors for dyspepsia are smoking, anxiety, and history of childhood physical or sexual abuse.[44]

Most men at the time smoked. We cannot likely know about childhood abuse. But as for anxiety, well, the young man was a scout pilot in the First World War. Other pilots, including A.H. Lofft from our photo, suffered gastrointestinal problems as a result of flying stress.[45]

Based on modern research into the effects of combat stress on pilots, we now know that an individual's ability to deal with stress is complicated, but among the factors are the morale of the unit and how well received an individual is among his peers. It should be noted that the leader of the squadron, for most of the time Walton was there, was Christopher Draper. Draper was removed from Naval 6 on June 6 because his presence was "detrimental to unit morale."[46] The report of Draper's superior officer is interesting.

> Acting Squadron Commander Draper although an exceptional fine pilot and very "full out" as regards flying at an Aerodrome for the edification of onlookers, making a great noise in the Mess at nights and leading conviviality generally; yet after six weeks in this squadron, he has produced no results.
>
> Both in his talk and in his actions, he exerts a depressing influence on other pilots—frequently asserting the weakness and inferiority of our machines, declaring that it is madness to attack a two-seater and so on. As regards actions, there has been a considerable and frequent increase in drinking since his advent, on nearly all occasions he is the leader. This officer has a bad influence on this squadron.[47]

Morale is affected by, among other things, the ability of the unit to carry out its job effectively. Yet later history suggests that Draper alone was not the cause of the squadron's problems nor Walton's. There may have been a downward spiral caused by mechanical failures, combat losses, bickering, and resentments. Walton's lack of discipline may have been his own mind's reaction to the stress of flying. We should give him the benefit of the doubt.[48]

Arthur McBurney Walton came from a privileged background, but despite being a good pilot, ran into problems once in the RNAS. ROYAL AERO CLUB AVIATOR'S CERTIFICATES, 1910–50

An observer and pilot—a man who appears later in this story as well—was one of the famous war poets of the time and among the first to try to tell in poetic form what it was like to fly and experience war in the air. He was twice treated for flying stress. An excerpt from one of his poems, "The Horrors of Flying," featured in his book *The Dawn Patrol and Other Poems of an Aviator*, reveals much.

> And now Imagination brings
> Its evil thoughts—I watch the wings.
> And wonder if those wings will break—
> The tight-stretched wires seem to shake.
> I see the ghastly, head-long rush,
> And picture how the fall would crush,
> My helpless body on the ground,
> With haggard eyes I turn around
> And contemplate the rocking tail,
> My drawn and sweating cheeks are pale.
> Fear's clammy hands clutch at my heart!
> Each second my existence ends
> In my disordered mind, whose pace
> I cannot check—its cog-wheels race,
> Like some ungoverned, whirring clock,
> When, frenziedly, it runs amok.

Flying in the First World War meant endless stress, and although some bore it better than others, all were affected. It certainly looks like Walton was ill.

"Caused a Disturbance"
Rod McDonald, Alex Knight, Stan McCrudden

As the young men at the Curtiss School passed their RAC certificates, they were sent to England in small groups, about once a week. Records show that Roderick McDonald and Stan McCrudden arrived at the Crystal Palace in London for induction on 17 September. Knight arrived two weeks later, but all three proceeded through their training as pilots together, first at Cranwell, then at Dover. They were posted together to Naval 8 Squadron based around Dunkirk, France. In our photo, McDonald is on the left side not far from Walton. McCrudden is on the right, not far from Gagnier. Knight is sitting centre, on top of the aircraft motor. Does that that tell us anything about him?

The three young men, far from home and engaged in a dangerous business, were friends and got into trouble together on 26 January 1917 at Cranwell. An identical statement appears in each of their RNAS records.

26-01-17. Report of misconduct in causing a disturbance with other officers at night in Duty Officer's Cabin in consequence of which he is to be deprived one month's seniority.[49]

Whatever the disturbance was, it was a minor infraction and the penalty, for high-spirited young Canadians interested in fighting a war and not in a career in the RNAS, inconsequential.

With the Finest—Naval 8

The squadron that these three young men joined in early 1917 was quite different in many ways from Naval 6. Morale was excellent as was leadership. It flew different aircraft: the Sopwith Triplane until the summer of 1917, then the superior Sopwith Camel. These machines gave Naval 8 pilots a distinct advantage in fighting, compared to their friends in Naval 6 with the troublesome Nieuport. Naval 8 was, in fact, the most successful of all the RNAS scout squadrons. When the RNAS and RFC were amalgamated on 1 April 1918, Naval 8 became 208 Squadron, Royal Air Force. During the

Stanley McCrudden, newly registered with the Royal Aero Club. ROYAL AERO
CLUB AVIATOR'S CERTIFICATES, 1910–50. COURTESY ROYAL AERO CLUB TRUST

whole war, Naval 8/208 pilots scored 298 victories in 565 air combats.[50] Good pilots would do well with this group, and McDonald, McCrudden, and Knight were good pilots.

One of its pilots, Australian R.A. Little, had arrived at Naval 8 with adverse confidential reports similar to those of Walton. One said, "As an officer he is quite hopeless and likely to remain so. He is to be informed that, if a further adverse report is received, his commission will be terminated."[51] What probably saved Little from the same fate as Walton was that Little was sent to Naval 8. He rapidly improved with the squadron and became a leading ace, with thirty-nine victories while with Naval 8 (and forty-seven overall). McCrudden, Knight, and McDonald were lucky in their posting.

Stanley Harry McCrudden was born in Toronto in 1891, so he was age twenty-five in our photo, and one of the older students. Despite the "incident" at Cranwell, he was rated as a very good pilot and officer. In the early days with Naval 8, he was described as "Very slow and lacks the qualities for command, but is keen and improving."

McCrudden flew constantly during the summer on offensive patrols. On 5 September 1917, while landing in a thick mist after a patrol, he crashed his plane and was severely wounded in the head.[52] This was serious enough that, in September, he was sent back to Canada on sick leave and kept there until February 1918. At one point, the RNAS considered having him stay there and assigning him to the Royal Flying Corps in Canada as an instructor, but he was passed fit for active duty and sent back to France to be an instructor at Vendome in France. There, his commander rated him a "Very capable and hard-working pilot instructor." McCrudden survived the war and returned to Canada.

Alexander Knight, the second high-spirited Canadian from the Curtiss School to be involved in the Cranwell incident, was called "Noisy" by his fellow pilots. Given how lively so many of them were, he must have been high-spirited indeed. Knight was born in 1893 in Collingwood, Ontario.

Alexander Knight rapidly matured as a pilot. ROYAL AERO CLUB AVIATOR'S CER-
TIFICATES, 1910–50. COURTESY ROYAL AERO CLUB TRUST

The archival records trace Knight's flying career and the changes in his confidential reports show how the war affected him. They also show that he grew in maturity and in leadership skills in Naval 8.

Cranwell, 21-1-17	V.G. Pilot indeed. Indifferent as an officer.
Dunkirk, 30-4-17	Drove down hostile machine out of control.
Dunkirk, 25-6-17	Good level headed Officer. Requires more experience and confidence. Fair fighting pilot.
Dunkirk, 28-6-17	Drove down hostile machine out of control.
Dunkirk, 6-7-17	Shot down enemy machine.
Dunkirk, 25-9-17	Good command and would lead a flight well. V. steady and reliable Scout Pilot.
Naval 8, 28-10-17	Has conducted himself to my satisfaction. A keen capable officer and a very good pilot.
Dunkirk, 28-11-17	Strongly recommended for promotion.

Two days after this last recommendation, Knight was declared medically unfit, but no specific ailment is recorded. He was allowed to return to Canada for sick leave, then in March was reassessed and found to be fit for duty. Knight returned to England in early April, just as the RNAS was combined with the RFC to form the Royal Air Force, and was assigned to duty as an instructor for the rest of the war.[53] This was a typical course of events for a physically and mentally exhausted pilot. With one confirmed and two "possible" enemy machines shot down, and as a successful Sopwith Triplane and Sopwith Camel pilot, Knight would be able to impart a lot of knowledge to the novice flyers. He was retained in the RAF until May of 1919, then returned to Canada. "Noisy" Knight served in the Royal Canadian Air Force in the Second World War on ground duties and died in 1947.

The only Maritimer in the Curtiss photo is Roderick McDonald, born in 1893, the son of Angus and Catherine McDonald of James

Roderick McDonald became an ace. He was killed in action and his body was never found. ROYAL AERO CLUB AVIATOR'S CERTIFICATES, 1910–50. COURTESY ROYAL AERO CLUB TRUST

River Station, Antigonish, Nova Scotia. Little is known about his background that would explain his being accepted as an officer, other than he was said to have mechanical ability.[54]

The confidential reports in McDonald's record tell us a bit about his career.

10-2-17	Cranwell.	V.G. Pilot and G. Officer.
21-6-17	Dunkirk.	Good level headed Officer. Improving rapidly as Officer and Pilot.
25-9-17	Dunkirk.	G. command. Very steady reliable Scout Pilot.
28-10-17	No. 8. Sqdrn.	Has conducted himself satisfactorily. A keen and capable officer and a very good pilot.
28-11-17	Dunkirk	Strongly recommended for promotion.
17-4-18	GOC 7th Brig.	Recommended for promotion to Flight Commander.
26-4-18	HQ RAF	Recommended for promotion to Captain, Flying, with effect from 18-2-18.[55]

In November 1917, McDonald was granted a month's leave and he was able to spend Christmas in Canada. He wanted more time off but that was denied, and he returned to duty. A rest definitely helped him deal with the stress, and the fact that he was given leave is an indication of the leadership of Naval 8. Many pilots in need of a rest did not have sympathetic squadron leaders.

McDonald was with the squadron on 9 April 1918 when a massive German attack broke through British lines, forcing a retreat. Naval 8 was ordered to evacuate their aerodrome but the weather was poor, and the Camels could not take off. Squadron Leader Christopher Draper ordered all eighteen Camel fighters to be stacked in the middle of the landing field and burned. The pilots and ground staff escaped in trucks.[56] Naval 8 was quickly re-equipped and again in the thick of fighting.

It has to be pointed out here that this Squadron Leader Draper was the same Draper who was removed from Naval 6 the previous summer when that squadron was not performing well and when Walton was having such difficulties. After the negative report on his leadership, Draper somehow recovered and was given command of Naval 8 in October 1917. Almost immediately he recognized that Knight was exhausted and sent him on leave. Despite Draper's failure at Naval 6, under his leadership Naval 8 continued to be an excellent unit. Nonetheless, Draper became known as the "Mad Major" because he flew under bridges to entertain watching troops. The factors causing success for a squadron and for a leader were complex.

McDonald was an ace, having shot down eight enemy aircraft. The Royal Air Force *Official Communique* described one of his victories.

April 21, 1918.

The weather was fine and the visibility good. 30 tons of bombs were dropped. Enemy aircraft were active but by no means aggressive. Two hostile machines were brought down by anti-aircraft fire—one falling in our lines, in addition to those brought down in combat.

Capt. R. McDonald, 208 Sqn, dived on an E.A. two-seater, firing 200 rounds from about 50 yards range and another 100 rounds at point blank range from below. The E.A. went down completely out of control and crashed beside a trench south-west of Henin-Lietard.[57]

This was the same day that the "Red Baron," Manfred von Richthofen, was shot down and killed.

Years later, the squadron armaments officer Lieutenant D.W. Pinckney remembered McDonald.

I remember good old Canadian McDonald as he climbed into his machine to do a real dirty job of work. He gave me a cheery grin and said,

Roderick McDonald in front of his Sopwith Triplane, Dusty II. Probably summer of 1917. RNAS pilots did well flying this nimble machine and helped regain air superiority that had been lost to Germany in April 1917.

"Guns all right Pinkie?"

"Think so."

"I'll just bet they are."

That was typical of Mac. Always the optimist, always cheery, and convinced that everything would be all right. Unfortunately, that flight was his last.[58]

Roderick McDonald was killed in action on May 8, last seen being pursued by two enemy aircraft. His body was never found, and he is commemorated on the Arras Flying Services Memorial in France.

Six Died

McDonald was the fifth of the Curtiss students to die.

The first to die was Sidney Emerson Ellis, there on the right side of the photo, between Reid and Johnson. He was twenty in the photo, twenty-one when he died. He was from Kingston, Ontario. He arrived in England a week before McDonald and was at Cranwell at the same time—although not involved in the "incident." Confidential reports say he was a keen and reliable officer, and a good pilot.

Ellis was posted to Naval 4 Squadron and became an ace. In the spring of 1917, he shot down two enemy aircraft and three more in July. He was in fact the second Camel pilot to shoot down an enemy aircraft. The Camel was perhaps the best British fighter of the war, but it was difficult to fly. While 413 Camel pilots died in action, 385 were killed in accidents. Ellis died on 12 July 1917 in an accident.[59] He was stunting, that is doing aerial tricks, when his Camel went into a spin, and he could not recover. Many of the high-spirited young pilots were constantly stunting. Another Canadian in Naval 4 at the time, the famous Roy Brown of Carleton Place, Ontario, commented in a letter home.

Sidney Ellis, arms folded to show the RNAS emblem on his sleeve. ROYAL
AERO CLUB AVIATOR'S CERTIFICATES, 1910–50. COURTESY ROYAL AERO CLUB TRUST

The trouble is stunting too near the ground. The number that are killed that way is awful. Sid Ellis who was at our home when he was a little kid was killed that way.[60]

Ellis was buried at the Adinkerke Churchyard Extension, at West-Vlaanderen, Belgium. The records of the Imperial War Graves Commission (now the Commonwealth War Graves Commission) show that his father, Reverend John D. Ellis of Smith Falls, Ontario, asked that the following inscription be carved on the headstone.

HE LOVED LIFE BUT HE LOVED GOD AND DUTY MORE

The second to die was also the youngest, at age nineteen. Malcolm Charlton Crerar (sixth from the right) was the youngest child of Peter and Marion Crerar of Hamilton. Peter, who died suddenly in 1912, had been a very successful lawyer and businessman, being influential in the development of the electricity system in Ontario. The family was very important in Canadian social circles, and Marion Crerar was a well-known philanthropist who actively supported the war effort. In 1915, she had donated the family mansion, Dunedin, to be a hospital for wounded soldiers. She operated the hospital privately, accepting only charitable donations and a dollar a day per patient from the City of Hamilton. "As long as my strength is spared," she said, "I am glad to do this for my war work... and for King and Country."[61]

Malcolm's oldest brother was Henry Duncan Graham, known as "Harry." In the Second World War, General Harry Crerar commanded First Canadian Army. Another brother, Alastair John, was also in the army. His half-sister Lillian had married Sir Adam Beck, founder of Ontario Hydro, the electricity generating company for the province, and was known as Lady Beck, cementing the family's social position.

Malcolm was educated at Highfield College School in Hamilton, where he was remembered for his "merry, sunny, disposition,"[62] and at Upper Canada College. He and Walton would have known each other. Following in the military footsteps of his older brothers, Malcolm had enrolled at the Royal Military College of Canada and entered in the fall of 1915. For the war, the cadets received just one year of training, and then entered the army. Malcolm's year had volunteered en masse for Imperial service—that is for the British Army. Malcolm was headed for the Royal Field Artillery (Harry was in the Canadian artillery) but faced one problem: at seventeen he was too young. That's when he entered the Curtiss Flying School. After he turned eighteen that summer, he was officially listed in the London *Gazette* as an officer in the Royal Field Artillery, but he never served with them.

We can trace some of Malcolm's early training, but the RFC records are not as detailed as the RNAS. He did attend the School of Military Aeronautics at the University of Reading and then seems to have been sent to Egypt for the rest of his training. After getting his wings, he was posted to 14 Squadron RFC, which was supporting the British campaign against Turkey in Sinai, Palestine, and Arabia. The German air force was supporting the Turkish Army. The RFC in the Middle East was equipped with aircraft that were obsolete in France. Their best machine was the Bristol Monoplane, which was fast and agile, but had a limited airtime duration and just one machine gun. The RFC had refused to send it to France; however, it was sent to the Middle East, and 14 Squadron got four early versions. It seems that 14 Squadron was acting as a test flight of the monoplane in combat.

Malcolm Crerar first appears in the squadron history on 29 June 1917, reported as flying a Vickers FB scout, acting as escort for aircraft spotting for the British artillery. On 7 July, at twelve thousand feet and on hostile aircraft patrol in the Vickers scout, Crerar shot down a German Rumpler aircraft. He was still just eighteen. On 1 August, he was reported in another combat with a German Albatros fighter. Then tragedy. On 3 August, he was flying a

OPPOSITE Malcolm Crerar's RAC photo. Learning to fly until he was old enough to go overseas with the Royal Artillery, Crerar chose the Royal Flying Corps instead. ROYAL AERO CLUB AVIATOR'S CERTIFICATES, 1910–50. COURTESY ROYAL AERO CLUB TRUST

ABOVE General Harry Crerar, standing left. Next to him is General Courtney Hodges, and then General Miles Dempsey. Front row, left to right are Field Marshal Montgomery, General Eisenhower, and General Bradley. BARNEY J. GLOSTER. CANADA DEPARTMENT OF NATIONAL DEFENCE / LIBRARY AND ARCHIVES CANADA / PA-3191506

Bristol monoplane, probably a test flight or familiarization flight, and crashed. His record says he died of wounds.[63]

In Canada, the death of the son of an important family got special mention in the press. The Toronto *Star* reported that he was "killed in an aerial battle with the enemy."[64] Other press coverage also suggested a death in aerial combat and also that he had been mentioned in dispatches for gallantry in the face of the enemy—his shooting down of an enemy aircraft. It may have been the hope that a young man, a youth, a boy, had died while fighting. The reality of an accident testing a controversial aircraft may have been kept from the family by 14 Squadron.

Malcolm Crerar was buried at Deir El Belah War Cemetery in Gaza, Palestine. He is also commemorated at Highfield School, Upper Canada College, and the Royal Military College of Canada. We can imagine the impact on his family and friends. His mother Marion died in 1919.

Harry Crerar directed that his brother's headstone be inscribed, THE HAPPY WARRIOR.[65]

The third to die was Ross Allison Blyth, seen on the right of the Curtiss photo, second from the end. He was from Toronto, born in 1892. He too was at Cranwell in January 1917, but his records state that he was "Dangerously ill with probably Cerebral Spinal Meningitis." He survived this but, in April 1917, was unable to fly because of otitis media, an infection of the middle ear. It was not until October of 1917 that Blyth was found fit for flying. He was declared missing in action and presumed killed on 23 January 1918, last seen going down out of control.[66] In mid-air, he had crashed into a German scout.

Blyth fell behind German lines and he was buried at St. Joseph German Military Cemetery. His family was informed of the location of his grave in 1923 by the Imperial War Graves Commission. His body was exhumed and reburied in a British cemetery—the Perth Cemetery (China Wall) at West-Vlaanderen, Belgium.[67]

The Bristol Monoplane was the future of aircraft design, but it was radical for its time and not trusted by the RFC command. CANADA DEPARTMENT OF NATIONAL DEFENCE / LIBRARY AND ARCHIVES CANADA / PA-006365

John Roy Allan, known as Roy in the service, was the fourth to die. He is ninth from the right, looking small next to the six-foot-five R. Marshall. Sidney Ellis is on the other side. Allan was from Westmount, Quebec, and had been a clerk at the Crown Trust Company in Montreal. He had also been a lieutenant in the Canadian Grenadier Guards, a Montreal militia unit. His RAC was issued on 20 July, and he was at the Crystal Palace in London on 27 August. He was recommended for seaplanes, being rated as a "Good officer and Pilot." In April, at RNAS base Manston, he trained on the huge Handley Page twin-engine bombers, not seaplanes. He was rated "A very keen officer. Good at handling men and excellent pilot." It is worth noting that two of the Curtiss class received an *excellent* rating as a pilot once overseas. The term *keen* appears twice more in his confidential reports as does the term *zealous* and *exceptionally good*.

Roy Allan's RAC photo, taken just after he graduated from the Curtiss School. He made a lasting impression. ROYAL AERO CLUB AVIATOR'S CERTIFICATES, 1910–50. COURTESY ROYAL AERO CLUB TRUST

Roy Allan was posted to Dunkirk to Naval 7 Squadron and in May was quickly taking part in bombing attacks on German aerodromes and ports in Belgium. Historian S.F. Wise described what Allan and fellow Curtiss school grad Frederick Ross Johnson experienced as soon as they arrived in France, as pilots of the brand-new Handley Page bombers.

> The first night raid was not until 10 May, when Flight Sub-lieutenants J.R. Allan and F.R. Johnson, both of Westmount, Que., flew two of the Handley-Pages. It is indicative of the shortage of experienced RNAS pilots that both returned to make their first night landing.[68]

Allan was awarded the Distinguished Service Cross for gallantry in many bombing raids, particularly that on 27 July 1917 on the German aerodrome at Ghistelles in Belgium. Allan's record shows that he had flown the following planes: Curtiss, Avro, BE2c, Bristol Bullet, and Handley Page. He made forty-three night bombing raids in Handley Page machines and three daylight raids.[69]

In April 1918, the British planned a daring raid on the port of Zeebrugge in German-occupied Belgium. They intended to block the harbour mouth by sinking old British warships filled with concrete, thus preventing German submarines (U-boats) from being able to put to sea. The whole area was well defended and had been the target of bombing attacks for years. The raid was scheduled for the night of 11/12 April. Naval 7 was assigned to bomb the harbour and to drop flares while the Royal Navy carried out the raid.

We are fortunate to have a description of the attack by Roy Allan's plane from one of his crew. Paul Bewsher was a pilot, observer, and navigator in the same squadron. He was also a poet of some renown at the time, having published a volume of poetry about aviation— one of the first on the subject. During the First World War, poetry was widely read, and the war poets became quite famous. After the war, Bewsher wrote his memoirs of his service as a night bomber and described in detail his flight as Roy Allan's observer and navigator that night. Bewsher had just returned to duty after four weeks treatment for neurasthenia—flying stress.[70] The impact of flying stress in apparent in his poetry and in his memoirs.

First machine—Pilot J.R. Allan, Observer P. Bewsher—bomb Zeebrugge Mole from 10:30 to 11:30—drop flares at 1 o'clock.

Roy Allan was a freckled, red-headed youth, brave, fearless, capable—easily the most popular man in the squadron—a pilot with a wonderful reputation as a night bomber; he has behind him the record of innumerable successful raids, when in spite of all difficulty, he has successfully driven home the attack. He was a Canadian from Montreal and the finest man I have met in the service. I was proud to have been given the opportunity to act as his observer.

Bewsher said that they were worried about the plan and the time in the air. He gave Roy Allan's reaction.

Hum. I've never been to Zeebrugge. An hour over the Mole sounds pretty beastly. What I don't like though is the wait—eleven thirty to one—that sounds foul to me. I have got the wind up! I don't know why! I don't like the idea somehow. I tell you frankly I'm windy about it.

Allan may have been afraid, but he did not hesitate to do his duty. After bombing the Zeebrugge Mole—a large, heavily defended artificial breakwater—Allan moved his huge bomber ten miles out to sea and flew in a waiting pattern. Then one of their engines failed, and they were too far from shore to make it back to England. Spotting a Royal Navy ship below, Allan ordered Bewsher to drop all the flares to get its attention and then landed in the sea nearby. Bewsher found himself under water.

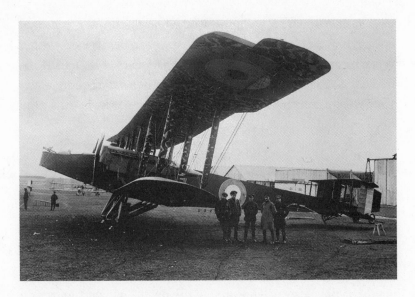

Advances in aviation technology since the flight of the Silver Dart in 1908 are obvious in this Handley Page O/100 bomber. The crew were still in the open and suffered from exposure during the long bombing and patrol flights.

LIBRARY AND ARCHIVES CANADA / PA-125413

> In sodden flying clothes, now terribly heavy, I found myself being dragged under the water as though some sea monster were gripping my ankles.

Bewsher grabbed the wing of the sinking machine and hung on until a navy launch arrived from the ship. The third member of the crew was Max Purvis, another Canadian making his first operational flight that night. He too was thrown from the machine but got back onto a part of one wing.[71] Bewsher was frantic.

> "Save my pal, save my pal. Where's Roy?"
> "He never came up."
> "Oh, save my pilot, save my pilot," I call out, bursting into sobs.

Bewsher's distress was increased when the Royal Navy rescuers told him the Zeebrugge Raid was cancelled because of weather. When he made it back to the squadron headquarters at Dunkirk, he found the squadron leader at breakfast with the wing commander. They were astonished to see him. Bewsher's memory of the situation is painful.

"Bewsher! Paul? Why – Why – where have you been? Where's Roy?"
"Roy, oh Roy! He's dead, dead in the sea, drowned in the wreck."
And throwing myself on a seat, I drop my face onto my arms on the table and burst into sobs.[72]

Then Bewsher said he remembered—a memory in pictures he said—a series of hospitals in France and then in England until he was in a convalescence hospital in the quiet English countryside. His official service record states that he was suffering from shock and confusion and concussion. Bewsher did not return to active service, obviously very badly injured in the mind. While recovering, he published a book of his own poems, *The Bombing of Bruges*, which included this one dedicated to Roy Allan. The pain is evident.

To Roy Allan
Died 11th April at Sea

Dear Roy! Who saved my life and lost your own
In that dark dreadful night above the sea
When you talked reassuringly to me
As we sailed lower—though you must have known
How great our danger was... then I was thrown
Swiftly into the water, whirling, free...
One thud of pain–a sudden agony–
And I came up... and found I was alone.
O how I cursed with madness when I knew

That you were dead beneath that wat'ry floor!
O how I wished that I, instead of you,
Had been ordained to return no more.
God must have rejoiced to take your hand
And have so good a soul to grace His land.

Bewsher, although wounded in the mind, kept very busy in England, publishing his book of poetry, then his war memoirs, *Green Balls*. He wrote for syndicated newspapers in the United States, and his description of aerial bombing appeared in newspapers in nearly every state. In 1919, he embarked on a lecture tour in the United States, recounting in dramatic fashion what it was like to take part in a night bombing raid. Bewsher then returned to his pre-war career as a journalist with the *Daily Mail* newspaper in London, having a long, successful career.

John Roy Allan's body was never recovered. He is listed on the Arras Flying Services Memorial, commemorating airmen with no known grave.

The last to die was John Playford Hales, aged twenty-three in the photo, standing seventh from the right. That relaxed group on the right side certainly look like they have become friends. Hales was known as Playford in Guelph, Ontario, west of Toronto, where he was born, but in the RNAS he was John. He had graduated from Guelph Collegiate Institute and then entered the Ontario Agricultural College in Guelph in 1910. He was on the college baseball team and was president of the Poultry Club. Hales graduated in 1915 with a Bachelor of Science in Agriculture degree and was immediately taken on staff at the college in the Poultry Department. OAC was a part of the University of Toronto, so the records there list him as a grad and staff member.

Although we see Hales at the Curtiss School in July, he did not get his RAC certificate until October. He only had fifty minutes, flying time by August, under Pilot Webber, and we know that progress was slow. He may also have been part of the program to have an extended stay at Long Branch to get more flying time. When Hales did finish at Cranwell in May 1917, he was rated a good officer and a very good pilot, recommended for scouts. He was first posted to coastal patrol in Scotland, then to Naval 9 Squadron in France, where he had a crash in July, injuring his legs. After recovery, Hales had four victories between September and November 23. His confidential report says, "Very keen officer," and "Strongly Recommended for Promotion."[73]

His record also shows that, from 17 July to 31 December 1917, he logged 247 hours flying. He was tired, but he was not sent on Christmas leave as McDonald had been. Instead, he was transferred to England and became a ferry pilot. He described his life in a letter to his brother Ernest.

Dear E.A., Wife, Family, Cat, Chickens etc.

Life over here is pretty good and I actually am a lucky fellow to be where I am. They don't work me too hard and they use a fellow on the level. I flew from Lincoln to London and tomorrow it will be London—Dover and Dover—London if the weather is OK. The new machines are pretty hot stuff and they handle well. A bit touchy on controls but real machines and the engines are wonderful. I love rotary engines. Flying cross country is just the very best way to see a place and I've seen a good deal of England, Scotland, France, Belgium, Holland, etc from the air. Some day I hope to fly over a good deal of Hunland proper.

I feel absolutely fit and full out but so far they seem content to let me have a good time and to fly the good busses around England. Really I don't mind although I know I should be in France but I'm willing to go just when and where they say.

Your splendid box of spies [apples] arrived in first class condition and they had the real good old flavor. Give all the kiddies my love and wish them all the fun possible. Now people I must scratch a few more notes, so heaps of love to you all and sweet, sweet dreams.

As ever,

Playford.[74]

In February 1918, he again asked for leave to Canada, citing nineteen months of continuous flying. His request was denied. However, from the letters, it sounds as if the time as a ferry pilot gave him needed rest. But life as a ferry pilot was not all easy. There was the danger of flying brand-new aircraft—factory fresh did not mean reliable. Also, there was a war on. During the big German attack in March 1918, Hales was involved in moving machines out of the way of the advancing German Army, and for this he was mentioned in dispatches, a military honour. In April he was promoted to captain.

In July, Hales was assigned to be a flight leader with 203 Squadron, RAF (formerly Naval 3).[75] This was another famous squadron, commanded by Canadian Raymond Collishaw, who was the leading ace of the RNAS and would end the war as Canada's second leading ace with sixty victories. He was a great leader as well as being a great pilot.

August and September were deadly for the RAF as they continuously attacked the German air force and the troops on the ground, supporting the 100 Days campaign that was defeating the German Army. Collishaw's squadron was assigned the job of strafing the German trenches.[76] The Camels had two Vickers machine guns firing through the propeller, and they could cause great destruction as they flew at low levels along the trenches. It was also dangerous work, generally disliked by the pilots. The unstable Camel was agile and quick turning in aerial combat, but prone to crash near the ground. And then there was German anti-aircraft fire.

The final letter Hales wrote home, on 15 August, tells us a lot about the stress and the danger. It is quite a contrast to his letter in February.

My hands are so cold I can hardly write straight so please excuse scribbling.

ROYAL NAVAL DEPOT,
CRYSTAL PALACE,
NORWOOD, S.E.

OPPOSITE, TOP The Ontario Agricultural College baseball team. Hales is seated second from right. This formal pose is quite a contrast to the relaxed students at the Curtiss Flying School. COURTESY UNIVERSITY OF GUELPH LIBRARY, ARCHIVES AND SPECIAL COLLECTIONS. RE2 OAC A259

OPPOSITE, BOTTOM Hales seemed to have a career in poultry ahead of him. Hales, President of the Poultry Club, is seated left. COURTESY UNIVERSITY OF GUELPH LIBRARY, ARCHIVES AND SPECIAL COLLECTIONS. RE2 OAC A119

ABOVE, LEFT Playford Hales, new graduate of the Ontario Agricultural College. COURTESY UNIVERSITY OF GUELPH LIBRARY, ARCHIVES AND SPECIAL COLLECTIONS

ABOVE, RIGHT A part of one of the letters of Playford Hales. COURTESY ARCHIVES AND SPECIAL COLLECTIONS, UNIVERSITY OF GUELPH. XR1 MS A519

Recently it seems I do nothing but write letters of sympathy. My pals are being killed on all sides and sometimes a fellow sits down and just wonders how he escapes. Fellows have been killed all around me and wounds are as common as flies in a jam factory. This year has seen real war raging on this part of the front and so much the terrible side of it that I am rather afraid it has made me more or less indifferent.

Our part has been dropping small bombs on infantry, machine gunning troops on the roads, in the trenches, and fighting all types of enemy aircraft. But we have the finest fighting machines in France, so are well prepared for our work. I have shot down another Hun machine and had heaps of indecisive fights and fights where machines went down out of control. It's a great game and I'm full out for it.[77]

His experience and his love of rotary engines did not save him. He was killed in action on 23 August. He was shot down leading his flight on a reconnaissance over the lines on the Somme front. Colonel Ray Collishaw reported flying over the crash site and seeing Hales's body being removed from the wreckage.[78] He would have written to the family in Guelph.

John Playford Hales is buried in the Meaulte Military Cemetery in France. His parents, Alfred and Catherine Hales of College Heights, Guelph, had the following verse engraved on his headstone.

LOVING AND KIND AS HE WAS BRAVE
FOR LOVE AND HOME HIS LIFE HE GAVE

Hales is still remembered every 11 November by his college. The Ontario Agricultural College built a new lecture hall in 1924 and named it Memorial Hall for the 109 students who had died in the First World War. Hales is named with the others on a bronze tablet. In addition to that is the commemorative silver rose bowl which still plays a central part of the annual Remembrance Day service. The silver bowl, filled with red roses, is solemnly brought into the ceremony and placed in a prominent place. The bowl was given to the OAC in memory of Playford Hales by his friend Kathleen Dowler Riter. She was an alumna of the Macdonald Institute, a women's college associated with the OAC. That college together with the Ontario Veterinary College and OAC formed the University of Guelph in 1964, which is now a major institution with thirty thousand students.

Seaplanes

So far, with the exception of Allan and Maclean, the pilots we have seen were all scout pilots, but the RNAS also posted many young pilots to seaplanes. This was not a secondary posting or an indication of any failing. They were in the navy after all. But the scout pilots tend to get the attention, especially the great aces. Seaplanes were based around the coast of Britain to defend the home islands from attacks from the sea and air, to hunt for submarines, to escort convoys, and to rescue crews from sunken ships and downed aircraft. Calshot, on the English Channel coast, was a major training centre. The Royal Navy was also a pioneer in basing seaplanes on ships and in developing the aircraft carrier so that scouts could be based at sea. The Curtiss Company developed several seaplanes that were bought by the RNAS. The Curtiss Large America H-12A had two Rolls Royce engines and a crew of four and could stay in the air on patrol for up to eight hours. As with all flying then, it was dangerous and stressful. They flew over the ocean out of sight of land, and many were lost to mechanical breakdowns, weather, or enemy action.

The Germans attacked the UK from the air using winged bombers, such as the Gotha, and the massive airships named for Graf Ferdinand von Zeppelin. Long before radar was invented, early

A.C. Reid   S. Ellis   R. Marshall   J. Crerar   J. R. Allan   R. A. Blyth
        F. R. Johnson   J P Hales   O. J. Gagnier   S McCrudden   H. M. Fitton

The deadly right side. Of the eleven men in this portion of the Curtiss class photo, five were killed, two wounded, and one became a POW. CROPPED FROM ORIGINAL ON PAGE 10. COURTESY OF TORONTO PUBLIC LIBRARY X23-4 CAB.III

detection of German attacks was difficult. Zeppelins and Gothas could appear suddenly over British cities and drop their bombs. They were also surprisingly hard to shoot down.

The most successful seaplane pilot in the war was Robert Leckie. He was born in Scotland in 1890 and went to Canada with his family. When the war started, Leckie went to the Curtiss School in 1915 to train on seaplanes, which the Curtiss school operated from Hanlan's Point on the Toronto islands. He was also one of the Curtiss students stranded in November 1915 when McCurdy closed the school for the winter season. Fortunately for Leckie, he was also one of those "rescued" by the Royal Navy, sent to England, and trained for the RNAS. He got his RAC certificate in May 1916.

In April 1917, Leckie was the pilot of the first Curtiss Large America to arrive at the RNAS seaplane base at Great Yarmouth. A month later, Leckie was on patrol (with his crew of three) over the North Sea when they spotted Zeppelin L22. Leckie flew his Large America to within fifty feet of the airship and his gunner opened fire. The L22 burst into flames and crashed into the sea. Leckie was awarded the Distinguished Service Cross for bravery. Leckie continued on patrols, making a hundred flights across the North Sea to the German coast, searching for aircraft, submarines, or surface ships.

Leckie was also credited with the sinking of a German submarine (after the war it was found to have survived) and, acting as a gunner on a land-based plane, he shot down another Zeppelin in August 1918. He was the only pilot to be involved in shooting down two Zeppelins.[79]

In September 1917, Leckie was on patrol over the North Sea when he tried to rescue the crew of a crashed bomber. His Curtiss Large America was damaged and could not take off again. The other crew was rescued but there was no way to communicate, other than through four carrier pigeons. They sent off their location and then drifted for three days. One pigeon made it back to base but died of exhaustion. The message however did get through and Leckie and the crews were rescued. Pigeon N.U.R.P/17/F.16331 was stuffed and is on display at the RAF Museum. The display reads, "A gallant gentleman."[80]

After the war, Leckie returned briefly to Canada to head up operations at the new Air Board and was part of the team that made the first flight across the country. He then returned to Britain and had a long and distinguished career in the RAF before returning to Canada in the Second World War and becoming chief of staff of the RCAF.[81]

In our photograph, four men served in seaplanes: "Pilot" MacLean, Reid, Fitton, and Marshall. Reid and Marshall appear later in this story.

Horace Cecil Malone Fitton of Simcoe, Ontario, became a seaplane pilot and instructor at Calshot, flying from bases in England for the whole war. In our photo, he is standing last in line on the right. He was twenty-four years old. He got his RAC certificate in mid-August and followed the usual route. At Cranwell he was rated as a "V.G. Pilot. Good and Keen officer." His service record actually gives the results of his final examinations at Cranwell, with 79.8 per cent in Navigation, 76 per cent in Gunnery, and 78 per cent in Wireless and Photography. These were very good marks, and Fitton was recommended for seaplanes.

He trained at Calshot where he was again rated as a "Good Pilot. G. and Reliable Officer." While stationed at Calshot, he met Gladys Bosworthick of Southampton, England, a city close to several seaplane bases. They married when the war ended and returned to Canada. He had worked for the Canadian Bank of Commerce before going to the Curtiss School, and after the war became a furniture factory owner in Southampton, Ontario. He died in 1947.

It is also most likely that Fitton, Reid, and Marshall kept in touch, as they all were trained or served at the seaplane base at Calshot. They must have commented, much as Hales did in his letters home, on the difference between the Curtiss JN-3 in Toronto and the Curtiss Large America seaplanes that they were flying.

A Keen Group

They did very well as pilots, our young men from the Curtiss School. In basic flying training at Cranwell and other basic flying establishments with the RNAS, the ratings in confidential reports are quite terse. In some records there are examination results, expressed as percentage marks, such as 66 per cent. A summary from their confidential reports shows:

- 12 Very Good pilots.
- 5 Good pilots.

Fitton was one of three men in the Curtiss photos who became seaplane pilots. They spent hours at a time on patrol searching for Zeppelins, submarines, or the German fleet. It was physically exhausting and dangerous. ROYAL AERO CLUB AVIATOR'S CERTIFICATES, 1910–50. COURTESY ROYAL AERO CLUB TRUST

A Curtiss Large America. It was quite a different kind of flying machine from the Curtiss JN-3s in Long Branch. It is very likely that Fitton, Marshall, and Reid flew this type of aircraft and served together at Calshot.

A painting of L22 being shot down. PAINTING BY HENK UITSLAG

At Cranwell and the other basic flying schools in England, the young men were also rated as officers. We don't have the criteria, if any were ever stated, but the senior officers wrote:

- 9 "Good officer."
- 2 "Fine officer."
- 2 "Moderate officer."
- 2 "Promising officer."
- 1 "Indifferent officer."

Two were described as "keen" while at Cranwell—Gagnier and Ellis. Quite a few others were rated as "keen" once they got to squadrons. There was a lot of meaning in that single word.

We have already seen that some high-spirited young men broke or bent military laws or regulations—the Cranwell incident in January 1917. Two others were convicted in a court martial for failing to diligently censor the outgoing letters of enlisted men. Acting as a censor was a much-disliked duty. The penalty was minor.

One young man, while still training at Cranwell, was admitted to hospital with gonorrhea. Once recovered, he was then severely injured in a training accident at Cranwell, and after getting out of hospital again, was given a month's leave in Canada. Upon return, he was found to have syphilis and again treated in hospital. At this point, he offered to resign but was allowed to stay on. He then had another crash in late 1917 and was in and out of hospital until finally allowed to go home on a long sick leave. He relinquished his commission "due to ill health" in July 1918. The air services seem to have been quite forbearing of some young men. Venereal disease was very common among the troops overseas, with 66,083 Canadian soldiers having been treated for VD by the end of the war—15.8 per cent of the Canadian Expeditionary Force.[82]

The Fatality Rate

"Casualty rate" is a term that covers the number of soldiers that are killed, wounded, become prisoners of war (POWs), or removed from combat effectiveness by sickness. As casualties they are removed from the war effort, from the fighting ability of the military. Records show that nineteen of the Curtiss students in the photo served overseas with the RNAS or RFC. Add the two instructors who had served in 1915 and we have twenty-one who served overseas. Six were killed, three wounded, two became POWs, and six were discharged ill or removed from combat operations as a result of illness. The casualty rate was seventeen of twenty-one, or 81 per cent.

An astounding number.

Take a look again at our Curtiss School photo, at the young men just learning to fly and their instructors. The casualty rate for the twenty-nine standing there is 59%. That does not include Webber, who was removed from the service because he could not be a gentleman.

Six were killed. The fatality rate for the nineteen students who served overseas was 32 per cent.

Medals for Bravery

The Dunkirk Town Council awarded a medal to Norman Douglas Hall for shooting down an enemy aircraft over the town on 2 May 1917. This was not a recognized British Empire decoration, but his actions impressed Dunkirk.

There was no medal at that time for being mentioned in dispatches, but the person mentioned in an official report for gallantry in the face of the enemy was entitled to wear a bronze oak leaf on another medal ribbon, and they got a certificate.[83] Mentions in Dispatches (MID) were, and still are, real honours given for bravery.

Malcolm Crerar, Playford Hales, Alfred Hartley Lofft, Robert Franklyn Abbott, Archibald Cumberland Reid, and Frederick Ross Johnson were mentioned in dispatches. That is six of nineteen students who served overseas. Crerar and Hales have already been described. The stories of the others in the photo make the group even more remarkable.

Robert Franklyn Preston Abbott was from Carleton Place, Ontario. In the photo, Abbott is fourth from the left. He had accumulated 372 minutes of flying time by 8 August, but he passed his RAC test in November 1916, so he likely took advantage of the program to allow some pilots more minutes.[84] At Cranwell he was rated "V.G. Pilot. G. Officer." He was posted to Naval 3 where he was rated "a daring fighter," and was mentioned in dispatches in August 1917 "for good work while with Naval 3 Squadron in the field." This is somewhat understated. He in fact had taken off from Dunkirk, France, and was on patrol over the English Channel with his squadron when they spotted German Gotha bombers heading to England. Abbott gave pursuit up to 15,000 feet (4,570 metres) and chased a Gotha bomber as far as Harwich, England, then had to land for fuel. A few days later he sprayed five hundred rounds into German hangars at Uytkerke Aerodrome from a mere fifty feet (fifteen metres).[85] In August 1917, he "sustained in action a penetrating wound above the femur. Permanent affects very severe."[86] He was totally disabled for seven months and then allowed to return to duty for short flights. Abbott survived the war.

Alfred Hartley Lofft of St. Mary's, Ontario, is just to the right of centre in our photo, in a white shirt, relaxed with his arms on the shoulders of Hunter and P. Jenckes. He was considered a very good pilot and good officer at Cranwell. He was kept on home service as a scout pilot and instructor. As an instructor at Manston, he was rated as "keen" with "Good Command." He was mentioned in dispatches "for good service during a raid by hostile aircraft on London, 7-7-17. Fought enemy machine as far as Walcheren Island

[Holland]." [87] That was a long, dangerous aerial combat and pursuit—then he had to get home. In January 1918, Lofft was declared unfit because of a duodenal ulcer and discharged from the RNAS. Today, we can assume that flying stress had contributed to this illness. Another victim.

Archibald Cumberland Reid of Winnipeg was one of the older students at the Curtiss School, born in 1889. He may have been older but does not look it—the handsome blonde man on the left side, next to Sidney Ellis. Reid graduated from McGill University in Montreal in 1910 with a BS degree. This was before Oliver Gagnier arrived at McGill, but the two must surely have swapped stories of campus life while waiting their turn to fly in Long Branch in the summer of 1916. Reid had been a structural engineer before entering the Curtiss School. He was also married. He got his RAC on 1 August, before Gagnier and the others already covered, but he developed appendicitis in Toronto and was delayed in getting to England. He overlapped at Cranwell with his Curtiss classmates who were involved in the "incident." Although not a part of that disturbance, he did something that produced a rating: "G. Pilot but overconfident and careless. G. Officer." That seems an unusual judgement.

Reid was recommended for seaplanes, and immediately overcame that dubious rating. "Finished seaplane course. V.G. pilot indeed. He did well in all subjects. A thoroughly reliable officer. Keen, Reliable officer. Strongly recommended for promotion." [88] Reid served as a navigation and compass officer as well as pilot. He began patrolling the North Sea with Naval 17. On 28 July 1917, he "Brought down an enemy machine in pieces." Reid was mentioned in dispatches twice. [89] He was also awarded the Air Force Cross in 1918, an award created in June 1918 to recognize valour, courage, or devotion to duty while flying, but not in combat. [90] Reid was promoted to captain and survived the war.

Roy Allan, already described, had been awarded the Distinguished Service Cross for his bravery in flying Handley Page

bombers. He and Frederick Johnson had trained together at Curtiss, Cranwell, Chingford, and Manston and had been posted to Naval 7. They piloted bombers on the same missions. Both appear in the history of 7 Naval Squadron, for example, as pilots in an attack on St. Denis Westrem and the Bruges docks in Belgium on the night of 5/6 December 1917.[91]

Frederick Ross Johnson is standing next to Marshall on the right side of the photo. His confidential reports are full of terms such as "Very keen, zealous, capable, good at handling men, sound technical knowledge, ability to command." Yet he pled guilty in a court martial for assisting another officer to evade admiralty regulations for censorship of men's correspondence. Although the young officers hated their role as censors of the letters of the enlisted men (or naval ratings), it was their duty. Johnson was reprimanded.[92]

After learning to fly at Cranwell and Chingford, north of London, he was sent to Manston to learn to fly Handley Page bombers. Posted to Naval 7 in the Dunkirk area, Johnson was mentioned in dispatches for "good work" in a bombing attack on a German aerodrome in August 1917. In fact, the good work was spotting a German bomber as it was landing and diving on it so that his observer could shoot it down.[93] A few weeks later he was awarded the Distinguished Service Cross,

> For conspicuous gallantry and devotion to duty in a bombing raid on Thourout Railway Station on the night of 20th–21st September 1917 when he came down to 3000 feet and made particularly good shooting [bombing].[94]

Johnson and Roy Allan had become friends at the Curtiss Flying School, trained together in England, and served together in Naval 7 flying Handley Page bombers. Roy Allan named his bomber "Kewpie Doll" and both pilots had a Kewpie Doll painted on their bombers.[95] Kewpies were extremely popular American story and comic strip characters, and the children's doll of the characters were first made

A.C. Reid was married and older than his Curtiss fellows. He was awarded the Air Force Cross for outstanding service. ROYAL AERO CLUB AVIATOR'S CERTIFICATES, 1910-50. COURTESY ROYAL AERO CLUB TRUST

in Germany. There were also pop songs about the Kewpies. We don't know exactly what Johnson and Allan were up to with Kewpies, but they had fun.

After the amalgamation of the RFC and the RNAS, 100 Squadron RAF specialized in night bombing, and Johnson was one of its lead pilots. The progress made in the development of aircraft can be illustrated by the change in how the RAF attacked. Throughout the spring, summer and fall of 1918, 100 Squadron made night attacks on targets in Germany—Saarbrücken, Hagendingen, and Friesdorf. On the night of 15/16 August, while flying over Germany, Johnson spotted a German bomber landing below him, dived his bomber down, and his gunner/observer shot it down.[96] On the night of 16/17 September, one of the engines on Johnson's Handley Page bomber failed, and he had to land in Germany. He and his crew tried to evade capture for two days but were caught on their way to Switzerland and became prisoners of war. Released after the war ended, Johnson returned to Canada and married Elsie Irene Eveleigh of Montreal in 1920.

Prisoners of War

Johnson spent only a few weeks as a POW. The previous summer, Norman Hall had been forced down behind German lines and spent the last year of the war as a POW in Karlsruhe, Germany. In the photo, Hall is on the left, in a dark shirt, between Walton and McDonald. He was nineteen at the time, from a prominent family in British Columbia. His father was both a dentist and a doctor, had been a member of the British Columbia provincial legislature, and was, in 1916, himself in the army, serving in the Canadian Army Medical Corps in Esquimalt, BC, on Vancouver Island. Norman passed his RAC near the end of August 1916 and, at Cranwell, was rated as a "promising officer and good Pilot."[97]

Prisoners in Karlsruhe later remembered that the food was terrible, but the American prisoners had their own canteen with

Military pilots are still painting their aircraft with personal art statements, with much attention by collectors focused on the Second World War. Johnson and Allan and other pilots also sang the Kewpie songs out of sheer fun at parties in the officers' mess. COURTESY THE LESTER S. LEVY SHEET MUSIC COLLECTION, SHERIDAN LIBRARIES AND UNIVERSITY MUSEUMS, JOHNS HOPKINS UNIVERSITY. BOX 53, ITEM 154A

LEAVES FOR ENGLAND

Sub.-Lieut. Norman Hall, of This City, Graduates From Curtis Aviation School, Toronto.

Sub.-Lieut. Norman Hall, son of Dr. G. A. B. and Mrs. Hall, of Yates street, this city, who has been receiving instruction in the Curtis Aviation school, Toronto, for the past three months, completed his course a week ago last Wednesday, and left this morning for England. He will be attached to the Royal Naval Aviation Service, and expects to go into active service in the immediate future.

The young airman is only nineteen years of age. He was born at Nelson, B. C., and removed here with his parents when he was still quite a young boy, attending the local public schools here. He graduated from the Victoria High school, passing his matriculation exams last year. He was always very interested in things mechanical, and had thought of going in for mechanical engineering if the call of Empire had not directed his thoughts to an imperative and definite career for the present in the service of his country. Sub.-Lieut. Hall is the eldest of three brothers. He successfully passed all the aviation tests at the Toronto Flying school last week.

AT KARLSRUHE CAMP

Good News From Flight-Lieutenant Norman Hall Reaches Parents.

Major G. A. B. Hall, M. D., last evening received a cable through the Berne Bureau of the British Legation that his son, Flight-Lieut. Norman Hall, who was reported some time ago as missing, is well and is a prisoner of war at Karlsruhe camp.

Dr. and Mrs. Hall wish to extend their thanks for the many kind in-

LIEUT. NORMAN HALL

quiries received since the announcement was made that their son was missing.

The young flight-lieutenant was educated in the local schools. He was born at Nelson 20 years ago, and joined the Royal Naval Air Service a year ago last May, and after being sent to France was attached to an aerial station at Luxeuil, near Belfort, where Lieuts. Beasley and Macdonald, of Victoria, were stationed for some time. He was later moved to the British front in Northern France.

ABOVE, LEFT Flyers often received special attention in the press, as these articles show. ORIGINALLY PUBLISHED IN THE VICTORIA DAILY TIMES, 2 SEPTEMBER 1916. A DIVISION OF POSTMEDIA NETWORK, INC.

ABOVE, RIGHT ORIGINALLY PUBLISHED IN THE VICTORIA DAILY TIMES, 25 SEPTEMBER 1917. A DIVISION OF POSTMEDIA NETWORK, INC.

OPPOSITE Norman Hall. ROYAL AERO CLUB AVIATOR'S CERTIFICATES, 1910–50. COURTESY ROYAL AERO CLUB TRUST

condensed milk, cigarettes, biscuits, chocolate, and other delicacies which they shared with other POWs.[98] Officer prisoners were treated better than enlisted men. Hall was released from captivity in December 1918 and returned to British Columbia. He then studied medicine at McGill University, graduated in 1926, and set up his practice in Nanaimo, on Vancouver Island, where his father Dr. George A.B. Hall was also in practice. Two of Norman's brothers also became doctors, and the four Doctors Hall were important members of the Nanaimo community. Norman Hall later qualified as a surgeon and moved to Alaska, where he married. He served as a major in the US Army in the Second World War and then set up practice in Phoenix, Arizona.

The Rest

Gordon Douglas Eckardt of Vancouver chose the Royal Flying Corps instead of the RNAS and served in Egypt and Salonica in Greece as a scout pilot. In October 1918, he was hospitalized with endemic typhus fever. He recovered and was discharged from the RAF. The RFC and RAF records are quite uninformative compared to those kept by the Royal Navy, so we do not have the confidential reports about Eckardt.[99] After the war, he tried his hand at flying and barnstorming. In 1920, Eckardt formed a flying business with another RAF pilot named J.L. Drummond on a farm near Aylmer, Ontario. They would go to fairs and other events to put on a show and take paying passengers for flights, charging ten dollars for twenty minutes in the air. Their enterprise ended when Drummond crashed at a fair in Shawville, Ontario, and the passenger was killed.

For a few of the young men, the trail has, thus far, gone cold. For Jenckes and D.H. Woollatt, there are no military records. The Royal Aero Club registry for Woollatt gives a licence number of 3396, one after McDonald and one before Gagnier, but there is no photo. For

LEFT Eckardt enjoyed the sights and delights of London in December 1916, as reported in the diary of another Canadian pilot, Harold Price. Price, a religious youth, did not approve. Price said, "Their standards and ideals are too low for me to be intimate friends with them."[100] Eckardt survived the charms of London. ROYAL AERO CLUB AVIATOR'S CERTIFICATES, 1910–50. COURTESY ROYAL AERO CLUB TRUST

RIGHT Jenckes disappears from records after learning to fly at the Curtiss school. ROYAL AERO CLUB AVIATOR'S CERTIFICATES, 1910–50. COURTESY ROYAL AERO CLUB TRUST

Paul Worthington Jenckes, there is only his RAC registration (3837) and photo. We get his full name but no other biographical information. He was registered on 10 November 1916, right at the end of the flying season.

H.H. Booth and W. Bryans appear in the military records in 1918, joining the Royal Air Force Canada and doing some partial training. They were still in flight training in Ontario on 11 November 1918. They had faced the dangers of flying—after all there had been 174 crashes in Canadian training from August to December 1918 that resulted in seventeen fatalities.[101] While their records may be slim, we know that flying of any kind was still dangerous. More about Canadian training in 1918 can be found in Parts Two and Three.

What Became of the Man Who Was Too Big?

G. Reginald Marshall, on the right in the photo, was born in Sheffield, England, and moved with his family to Toronto where the Marshalls started a spring-mattress factory and acted as agents for Sheffield hardware manufacturers. In flight training at Cranwell, he was considered a very good pilot and promising officer: "Should make a good scout pilot but is too big for this type, being 6'5". Recommended for Seaplane Pilot." Marshall did have a successful career as a seaplane instructor and pilot, mostly at the base at Calshot on the southern coast of England. There he almost certainly would have flown the Curtiss Large America seaplane. The comments in his confidential report are complimentary:

> Excellent pilot. Very Keen, hardworking, and likely to make good instructor. VG command indeed.
>
> A very capable instructor indeed and a very efficient officer. He is recommended for promotion.
>
> Excellent seaplane pilot and very keen. Hardworking and a good instructor. V.G. command indeed.[102]

Reginald Marshall married an Englishwoman named Lily, from Sheffield, and did not return to Canada save for business trips. His occupation stated on passenger ships lists is given as "steel merchant" in 1922 and "brush manufacturer" in 1929.

Conclusion

The photo should haunt us. There they stand, most smiling for the camera, and for us. Few had any real idea of what lay ahead—not even the veteran instructor—for the air war intensified and became more deadly than any could have expected in 1916. We now know a little of what happened to them. They were our people.

The Curtiss Flying School closed for good at the end of the 1916 flying season. The RFC and RNAS had decided to accept young men directly into flight training without a private licence and to do the basic training in house. The Long Branch school and the factory turning out Curtiss JN-3 machines were taken over by the Royal Flying Corps in 1917, and the training program was expanded with many new bases built around Southern Ontario. In fact, at the end of 1916, it is safe to say that training had just started and that the young men in our photo were trailblazers. That becomes the story in Parts 2 and 3.

Paul Bewsher, physically and mentally injured by the war, mourned the loss of his friend Roy Allan. He concluded his memories of the war and of those he mourned with this:

Infinitely remote, like a scarce-remembered dream, is the war to me today. I seem to have been a civilian, ever to have strolled at ease down sunlit terraces of London, through the drowsy hours of an English spring—but every night with the slow approach of azure twilight I feel a strange stirring in my heart. As the first primrose star blooms in the east, I seem to hear the roar of starting engines, and when, in cold and sublime beauty, a silver moon rides high in

G. REGINALD MARSHALL,
*who has recently passed his examination
for the Royal Naval Air Service, after
ten weeks spent in training at the Curtiss
Aviation School, Long Branch, Toronto.
He will sail for England in a few days.
Mr. Marshall is known to many in the
hardware trade. He has been for some
time associated with his father, Geo. A.
Marshall, 70 Lombard St., Toronto, re-
presenting a number of well known Sheffield manufacturers. The above snap-
shot was taken after Aviator Marshall
had descended from a flight in the neigh-
borhood of Toronto. A portion of the
aeroplane may be seen in the picture.*

This photo shows Marshall at the Curtiss School. The announcement from the trade paper *Hardware and Metal*, 7 October 1916, sheds some light on how Marshall may have met his wife. HARDWARE AND METAL. 7 OCTOBER 1916. P125

the vast immensity of the night, I yearn with almost an unbearable pain to be once more sitting far above a magic moonlit world, to be moving ever onwards through the dim sky.[103]

Youth Ascended.

2

YOUTH LOST

THE LIFE OF FIGHTER ACE LIEUTENANT OSBORNE ORR, DFC

The Wings are stretched: the mighty engines roar;

And from across this loved land I must depart.

PAUL BEWSHER
Crossing the Channel[1]

I am going to have the opportunity to die

as every brave man should wish to die,

fighting—and fighting for my country as well.

That would retrieve my wasted years

and neglected opportunities.

ELLIOTT WHITE SPRINGS
War Birds: The Diary of a Great War Pilot[2]

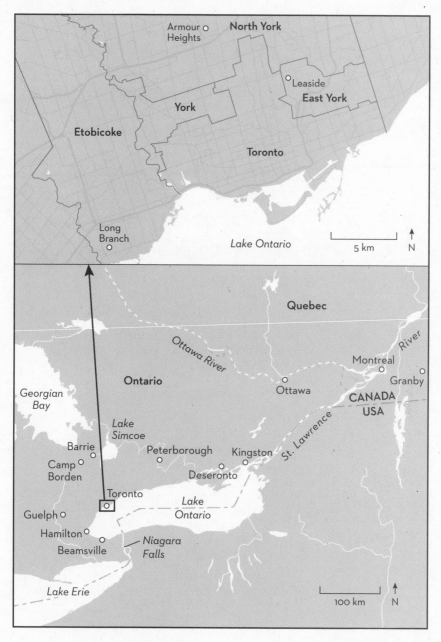

Southern Ontario and Quebec.

O N THE NEXT page is a remarkable picture that has survived for over one hundred years. The shaded eyes and solemn face are expressive. It is a portrait of Osborne Orr that his mother wore every day in a silver locket around her neck. He is in the uniform of a pilot in the Royal Air Force in 1918. This is the only colour picture of Osborne Orr, and it was commissioned for his mother, Caroline Stewart Orr. She was immensely proud of her son and must have thought of him constantly. When she died many years later, the locket was passed on to her sister, and has been kept in the family since then. It is a unique artifact and heirloom and reminder to us of the feelings of people now remote from us.

Lieutenant Osborne Orr served with the RAF in northern France. On the morning of 23 October 1918, Orr climbed into his Sopwith Camel fighter. Newspaper reports and Royal Air Force records tell us that the temperature was just six degrees Celsius but promised to

COURTESY JAMES THAYER

rise to fifteen. There was no rain in the forecast, but it was misty. His squadron, 204, was on a bombing mission behind the German lines. It was also a good day for fighter pilots to go aerial hunting. Orr checked the twin Vickers machine guns mounted in front of him and went through the start-up procedure. He was twenty-three years old.

It was just nineteen days before the end of the First World War. The German armies were in retreat, and Belgium was again free after four years of occupation. The German government had just approached American President Woodrow Wilson to try to negotiate an end to the war, but Britain and France had pressured Wilson to take a hard line. Surely, the end of the war was in sight.

In the Great War, as it was then called, a pilot became an ace when he had shot down five enemy aircraft. Lieutenant Orr had shot down his fifth nine days earlier, on 14 October, but poor flying weather in the days following had limited his opportunities for more. The pilots of the Royal Air Force were a special type, and the aces were the elite among them. The recruiting posters in Canada had appealed for a certain type of young Canadian to join up.

> Ideally, he should be between eighteen and twenty-five years of age, have matriculated from high school, and have spent a couple of years at university. He should be well grounded in algebra and geometry, be able to 'speak the King's English,' and bear 'the earmarks of a gentleman.'

As a staff officer told the Toronto *Mail and Empire*, "the type of fellow wanted as a pilot ... is the clean bred chap with lots of the devil in him, a fellow who had ridden horses hard across country or nearly broken his neck motoring or on the ice playing hockey."[3]

Today, well over a hundred years later, the language used seems quaint, but that reference to lots of the devil and ice hockey gives us some idea of what was wanted. Certainly, many of the photos from

Skilled trades were in as much demand as pilots.

the time show some cheeky looks among the young chaps standing beside their impossibly flimsy flying machines. But as delicate as those airplanes look, they were the fastest machines on the planet. Flying was a new adventure, and flying in combat had glamour that was denied the troops in the trenches. It was also dangerous—the average life expectancy of a combat pilot in 1917 was sixty-nine flying hours. Despite this terrible mortality rate, for many young men the call to be a pilot was irresistible.

We might assume that Osborne Orr had some of these qualities. Normally we would know about his character and personality from his letters, from memoirs, from what his family and fellow pilots remember of him. None of these are available. Despite being an ace, the life of Lieutenant Orr has grown somewhat obscure, so we will track him through official documents, newspaper accounts, and histories of the units he served with. Some surprises are in store.

Early Life and a Shocking Turn of Events

Osborne John Orr was born on 15 July 1895 in Nanaimo, British Columbia. His mother was Caroline Stewart, his father William John Orr. William was a partner in Orr & Rendell's Boot and Shoe Emporium on Commercial Street. After Osborne was born, the family moved from Nanaimo to Wellington, which is today amalgamated with Nanaimo but in the 1890s was a country location just north of the city. Osborne's sister Vera Eleanor was born there in 1898.

It may have been a natural match between William and Caroline, as she came from a family of merchants in Nanaimo. Her parents were immigrants from Scotland, and they had a very large family. Caroline was named after her mother, who bore seventeen children. William was born in Quebec. How he ended up in Nanaimo is not known. William had a twin brother, George Osborne Orr, who emigrated to the United States and became a dentist in St. Paul, Minnesota.

ABOVE THE DAILY TELEGRAM, NANAIMO, 8 APRIL 1894. P4. COURTESY UNIVERSITY OF BRITISH COLUMBIA LIBRARY

OPPOSITE Caroline Reid Stewart and her daughters in Nanaimo, around 1890. Caroline Stewart is front left. She and her son Osborne have a striking resemblance. COURTESY JAMES THAYER

Today, Nanaimo is a modern city of about a hundred thousand people and a regional centre on Vancouver Island. In the 1890s, only forty years after the first European structure went up, it was a frontier coal mining town. It was a rough but thriving place with a lot of single miners crowding the rooming houses and taverns. Miners were a hardy lot working a dangerous job, with many dying in mine accidents. Union activity produced increasing tensions with the coal mine owners and the middle class. But the young men of this tough mining town also won the provincial rugby and football championships in 1895. There were also a lot of Chinese and Japanese immigrants in Nanaimo, with the Japanese concentrating on fishing the salmon- and herring-rich waters. Immigrants from China were miners and business operators. Everyone needed shoes.

William Orr appears to have been an ambitious man, as the store advertised in newspapers in Victoria, the provincial capital 100 kilometres to the south, and he had ambitious plans. A brief announcement was made in 1897 that Orr and Rendell were about to open another store in Rossland, BC, 450 kilometres east of Vancouver. Instead, he branched out on his own shortly after that and moved his family to Vancouver and the new, growing east end. He opened his new store, William J. Orr, Boots and Shoes, at 420 Westminster Avenue, with the family living at 309 Westminster. The street became Main Street in 1910. There he prospered. The social pages of Vancouver newspapers recorded the presence of Mrs. William Orr at functions around the city and announced when she returned from vacation in Seattle. Osborne and his sister appeared also as guests at various children's birthday parties. The family eventually moved to the Point Grey neighbourhood.

Osborne was about six years old when the family moved to Vancouver. He attended Grandview School until 1911, when he passed the provincial high school entrance examinations. This was a significant event, and the names of all pupils in the province who passed were printed in the newspapers. In Canada at the time, the average educational level was just Grade 6. Osborne was fifteen, which would be old for entering high school today, but elementary school extended then to the end of Grade 9. Osborne attended the brand new Britannia High School on Commercial Drive. Attendance at high school in those days was quite an achievement, and completing high school, or matriculating, was rare. Very few Canadians attended university. In order to get enough recruits, the Royal Air Force in Canada would have to lower its university requirement and even take in young men who had not matriculated.

Osborne Orr did not matriculate. His name does not appear in the newspaper list of graduates for 1913 or 1914. Perhaps he had failed or lost interest. Certainly, something unusual happened in his life. Right at the end of the school year, United States Customs records show that he entered the US at Seattle on 22 June 1914. The record states that Osborne was a shoe clerk, his father had paid his passage, and his destination was the home of Dr. G.O. Orr in St. Paul, Minnesota. Business records in St. Paul for 1915 list him as a shoe salesman, so he was following the family business while staying with his uncle.

In the meantime, Canada was at war and hundreds of thousands of young Canadians voluntarily joined the army and went overseas to fight on the Western Front in France and Belgium. Orr was not evading conscription because there was no draft in Canada until 1917. At the same time, he did not return home to join up. We might assume that he had been sent to live with an uncle while he sorted out what he wanted to do in life. Any hint that Osborne was a troubled teen can only be guessed at. He came from a prosperous middle-class family and was living in St. Paul with his respectable uncle. What happened next is a surprise.

On 8 February 1917, Osborne J. Orr was arrested in Minneapolis, Minnesota, and charged with purse snatching. Two young men had attacked Miss Rose Smith and seized her purse with $4.75. On hearing her screams, two other young men living at the YMCA gave chase and captured Orr. His partner escaped but was later caught. In Orr's pocket police found a letter from his mother in Vancouver that said, "God grant that the $10 I sent you will tide you over until you can get some sort of work. May you come out all right."

The Minneapolis *Star Tribune* reported Orr waived a preliminary examination in municipal court and was bound over on a grand jury charge. Bail was set at three thousand dollars, but the accused could not furnish it. Orr is quoted as saying, "May mother never hear of this. I'll make good yet."

The search for records after so many years is often rewarding, but not in this case. The State of Minnesota Archives do not have anything about the trial. The county court records—in this case Hennepin County—are silent on Orr. Newspapers did not cover any later trial. Prison records are not available. Did Uncle George help? Was Orr convicted? Did the entry of the United States into the war a few months later have an effect on the charge and on Orr's return to Canada?

Then Virginia Thelma Kennedy appeared in the story. She was born in Akron, Ohio, in 1898, the youngest of five children. The 1911 US Census shows she was living with her family on the west coast, in Spokane, Washington. The social pages in Spokane newspapers list her as a guest at several children's birthday parties, so her life might have mirrored Osborne's. A State of Minnesota marriage licence was applied for by them in 1917, but never used. How they met and, indeed, why a girl from Spokane was in St. Paul in the first place are both unknown; answers are obscure as are the reasons why Osborne himself was in St. Paul at the time. It would make a good movie. As would what happened next.

Osborne and Virginia were married in Vancouver on 14 September 1917. The marriage certificate states that Osborne John Orr, Presbyterian, bachelor salesman, son of William Orr, merchant, and Caroline Orr of 2046 Beach Avenue, married Virginia Thelma

A sharply dressed Osborne J. Orr, before joining the RFC. COURTESY JAMES THAYER

36742

VITAL STATISTICS ACT.

SCHEDULE F.— Marriage Certificate.

Marriage solemnized in the District of .... B.C.

No.	947
Name and surname of bridegroom.	Osborne John Orr
Age.	22
Condition, bachelor or widower.	Bachelor
Rank or profession.	Salesman
Residence.	2046 Beach Ave.
Place of birth.	Nanaimo
Name and surname of father.	William J. Orr
Name and maiden surname of mother.	Caroline Stewart
Rank or profession of father.	Merchant
Religious denomination of bridegroom.	Presbyterian
Name and surname of bride.	Virginia Thelma Kennedy
Age.	18, 1⁄2
Condition, spinster or widow.	Spinster
Rank or profession.	At home
Residence.	504 Hastings St. E. Furrera Court
Place of birth.	Akron Ohio
Name and surname of father.	Samuel H. Kennedy
Name and maiden surname of mother.	Henzetta Proctor
Rank or profession of father.	Printer
Religious denomination of bride.	Episcopalian
Date of marriage.	Sept. 14 / '17

Married at * 504 Hastings St. E. Vancouver, B.C., according to the

rites and ceremonies of Baptist Church by † Licence

No. 58559

This marriage was solemnized between us { Osborne John Orr
Virginia Thelma Kennedy.

In the presence of { G. Walter Allen.
Miss Gail Page

(Signature of Minister or Clergyman) J. Willard Litch

* Enter place and situation.
† Banns or licence—give No. of licence.

10,000-6-17.

Kennedy, Episcopalian, spinster, daughter of Samuel A. Kennedy, printer, at 504 Hastings Street East, Vancouver. The marriage was conducted by J. Willard Litch, a prominent Baptist clergyman.

Why was the wedding not at her parents' home in Spokane? Why was there no announcement in any Vancouver or Spokane newspaper? The imagination runs wild, but the facts are few.

Then just eighteen days later, Osborne joined the Imperial Royal Flying Corps in Toronto. Mrs. Virginia Orr was with him. We cannot know all that was going on in this young man's life.

The Imperial Royal Flying Corps (IRFC) had established a recruiting office in Vancouver earlier in 1917 and advertised widely. If Orr applied in Vancouver, he would have been interviewed and given a medical examination. If he passed, the IRFC would then pay his train fare to Toronto for a more complete interview and examination. It appears that his lack of matriculation did not matter. He certainly did not reveal a criminal past—that would have disqualified him.

Joining the Imperial Royal Flying Corps

In 1916, the Royal Flying Corps was faced with a desperate need for more pilots and ground crew, and with a shortage of safe flying areas in the United Kingdom. They turned to Canada, but found a government fully committed to raising a large army and uninterested in an air force.

However, in the spirit of Imperial unity and support, the Canadian government did agree to allow the RFC to come to Canada and establish a large, separate training plan, recruiting Canadians and Americans. This Canadian-based operation was called the Imperial Royal Flying Corps.

When the Royal Air Force was formed in Britain in April 1918, the IRFC became RAF Canada. These names have caused some confusion in the twenty-first century, when Canadians are less familiar with our historical role in the British Empire, but in 1917, the Imperial Royal Flying Corps name clearly appealed to Canada's membership in the world's greatest empire.

The task facing the British officers who arrived here in January 1917 was immense. Few Canadians had ever flown—or even seen—an airplane. There was of course the Curtiss Flying School and Curtiss Aeroplanes in Toronto, and RAF bought these and quickly expanded. The job of building the infrastructure of the IRFC was given to the Imperial Munitions Board, which the British government had set up in Ottawa to produce weapons and ammunition in Canada. Toronto business leader Joseph Flavelle headed the IMB and used experienced Canadian business executives. So, while Ottawa was not interested in an air force, the IMB did supply the Canadian business expertise the IRFC needed to get started. The IMB bought or leased new factory space, sought out and leased farm fields to turn into aerodromes, and signed contracts for the construction of barracks, hangars, workshops, and hospitals. The IRFC, however, paid all the bills.

The IRFC was heartily welcomed in Toronto and Southern Ontario. The economic benefits as well as the contribution to the war effort were obvious. The Toronto Board of Education turned over the brand new Jesse Ketchum Public School as an induction centre for recruits. The University of Toronto provided student residences and classrooms. It was all an immense program and extremely high tech for its time. Thousands of new civilian jobs were created.

In 1917, the IRFC staff were British, but as months passed, more Canadians were trained and became staff in turn. Canadians already flying in Europe who had been wounded—or were in need of rest—were returned to Canada as instructors. By war's end there were so many Canadians it really was the RAF Canada.

Missing Records

Tracing the life of Osborne Orr to this point has meant following public records. Once he joined the IRFC his story became both clearer and frustratingly interrupted. The military usually kept detailed records which are available today to the dedicated researcher in digitized form, making it easier than ever before to find out about those who served. The records of the RFC and the RAF, and of all Canadians who served in them, are kept at the National Archives in London, England.

In 1919, RAF Canada's official history boasted that it had kept detailed records of every aspect of every cadet's training in Canada. Unfortunately, those records are lost. They are not in the UK National Archives. They are not in Canada. With Osborne Orr, the first entry in his UK Archive record begins with, "From Canada." The only part of his Canadian record to cross the Atlantic was his attestation paper. For most Canadians who joined the IRFC, even that is missing.

Archivists themselves are, by nature and profession, interested in finding and preserving important records. They have helped look for these missing records and provided valuable links and suggestions, but the consensus is that the IRFC service records are gone. Only a list of names survives. It is something of a national historical catastrophe that so many of the records of over twenty thousand Canadians who served in the First World War are missing.

Orr Becomes a Pilot

From Orr's attestation papers we know that he had lived on Beach Avenue in Vancouver, that he was a salesman (shoes, we assume), and that he was married, with his wife Virginia living at 30 Grosvenor Street,

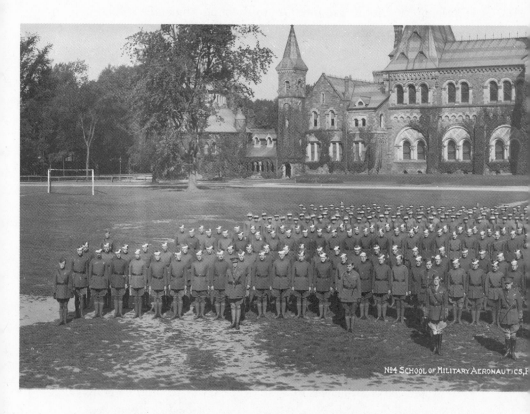

N⁰4 SCHOOL OF MILITARY AERONAUTICS, T

Cadets at the University of Toronto shortly before Osborne joined up. In the back rows are American cadets, in their distinctive hats. The building is University College, and on the right the brand new Hart House. Both look exactly the same today. MERRILEES, ANDREW / LIBRARY AND ARCHIVES CANADA / ECOPY 4474437

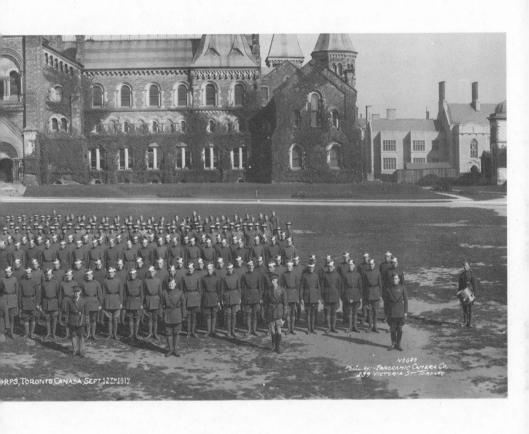

RPS, TORONTO, CANADA, SEPT. 12TH 1917

Photo by PANORAMIC CAMERA CO.
239 VICTORIA ST. TORONTO

Toronto. He was five foot eight inches tall (1.73 metres) with a chest measurement of 36 inches (0.91 metres). The fact that he was married was a little unusual, as the RFC did not think that married men made good aviators. In September 1918, the *Lancet*, then and now a renowned and respected medical journal, published an article on pilot selection by two RAF officers who said this of married pilots:

> The majority of successful pilots are unmarried, and our own observations tend to show that marriage is a definite handicap owing to the increased sense of responsibility.
>
> The married man has the knowledge of what his death may mean to his wife and family, and, moreover, has the opportunity of discussing it with his wife and manufacturing in his own home a condition of nervousness which eventually becomes so great that he confesses to his instructor that he has completely lost his nerve.

What were considered medical grounds for preferring unmarried pilots in 1918 did not apply so much in 1917, as the IRFC faced an extreme shortage of pilots. History would judge the accuracy of this "medical" analysis of married pilots.

Although the records of so many individual Canadians are lost, we can build a picture of what happened to Orr after October 1917 from the history of the IRFC. The most intriguing of these histories is the one written in 1919 by Alan Sullivan. *Aviation in Canada 1917-1918* is of such importance that it has been digitized and is available freely online. Sullivan served with the RAF Canada and was a famous author at the time. He provides great detail about the IRFC operations.

For the five months following his attestation, Osborne Orr would undergo intense training and see little of his bride. When Orr arrived in Toronto in October 1917, he would have immediately been sent to Jesse Ketchum Public School to be issued a cadet's

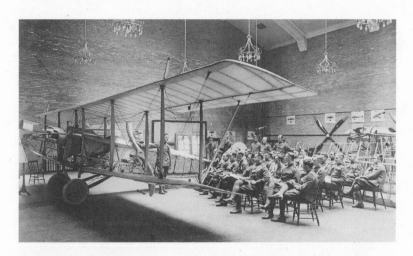

TOP Airframes class, No. 4 School of Military Aeronautics, University of Toronto. Cadets were given training that was high tech for its time. CANADA DEPARTMENT OF NATIONAL DEFENCE / LIBRARY AND ARCHIVES CANADA / C-020396

BOPTTOM Women overhauling an engine for a JN-4 Canuck. The IRFC and RFC-Canada hired and trained 1,200 women in Toronto and Southern Ontario. Alan Sullivan described their work as "a definite advantage of the Corps." CANADA DEPARTMENT OF NATIONAL DEFENCE / LIBRARY AND ARCHIVES CANADA / PA-022784

uniform and kit. Military discipline started—there were sergeants and corporals to drum military smartness into the new men. Cadets were then sent to the old Curtiss Flying School in Long Branch for further "enlightenment" about the ways of the IRFC. Although they may have had "the ear-marks of a gentleman," they had to learn how to be officers. The RFC was a part of the British Army and expected military discipline.

Osborne Orr's education as a pilot began at No. 4 School of Military Aeronautics on the University of Toronto grounds. Early in the war the RFC had realized that an intense scientific and technical education was essential to training good airmen. Schools of Military Aeronautics were set up at British universities, and at the University of Toronto. The twelve hundred cadets in each class were taught by RFC instructors. They lived in tents in summer on the university playing fields, and in the student residences in winter. The subjects were navigation, wireless, photography, instruments, engines, airframe, reconnaissance, and general military knowledge. The training was six weeks, the daily workload heavy, and examinations were constant. However, there was a certain leniency—those who failed were given several chances to retake courses and eventually pass. The pilot shortage was that severe.

After passing these courses, Orr would at last move on to flying instruction. The IRFC had built training facilities at Camp Borden, near Barrie, one hundred kilometres north of Toronto. Nearer the city were fields at Leaside and Armour Heights which have long since been swallowed up by the expanding city. There were two other training camps near Deseronto, two hundred kilometres east of Toronto and closer to Kingston.

All cadets learned to fly the Curtiss JN-4 (Can), called the Canuck. The IRFC adopted and then refined the American-designed JN-3 that had been built at the Curtiss plant in Toronto because it was a stable training platform—and available. Importing aircraft from Britain across a U-boat–infested Atlantic was not a good idea. Thousands of Canadian civilians were thus employed in the aircraft industry in production and maintenance, and all within less than ten years after McCurdy had made the first aircraft flight in Canada. The presence of the Imperial Royal Flying Corps gave Canada a big head start in the world of aeronautics.

The IRFC in Texas

The IRFC operation was vastly larger than McCurdy's Curtiss one. The RAF Canada official history shows that during the spring, summer, and fall of 1917, over five hundred pilots graduated and posted to England to undergo final training. But as winter approached the IRFC fully expected that flying hours would be much reduced or lost altogether. The best winter climate in Canada was on the west coast, so officers were sent to Vancouver to scout the situation. Land was leased near Vancouver, but upon further reflection, the IRFC realized that the heavily forested west coast would not be a good place for the student pilots who frequently crashed their delicate "Canucks."

Brigadier General Cuthbert G. Hoare, the commander of the IRFC, was not only energetic and efficient, but also a charmer who got along very well with Canadians and, as it turned out, with Americans. He had already started recruiting in the US, all against American law but allowed nonetheless with a wink from US officials. Hoare made an agreement with American authorities for the winter use of training facilities in Texas, near Fort Worth, in return for also training American pilots and mechanics. The US Army had very little experience in flying and looked on the deal as a winning chance to help rapidly expand their air force. The Aviation Section of the US Signal Corps provided two aerodromes for the accommodation of ten IRFC squadrons. The first contingents left Toronto in late September 1917, and by 17 November, two of the three training wings of the IRFC were operating in Texas.

The people of Fort Worth welcomed the Canadian and British airmen with open arms. With their exotic uniforms and foreign accents, the young men from the north made a hit. They were, in the slang of the time, "dashing." Around Fort Worth, dances, tours, and sporting events were arranged, and many newcomers were invited into local homes, especially over Christmas.

IRFC Star Attraction

Adding to the attraction of the IRFC was the presence of Vernon Castle, a famous Broadway theatre and silent film star. Castle was born in England and achieved fame with his American socialite wife, Irene. They performed as ballroom dancers on stage and in film, and popularized modern dances such as the foxtrot. Irene is credited with introducing the short hairstyle for women called the "bob," which became the fashion statement of "flappers."

Vernon Castle's English roots were strong, and when the war started, he wanted to fight for his native country. He paid for flying lessons in the US (then not at war), returned to the UK, and joined the RFC. He flew three hundred combat sorties and shot down two German airplanes. He was then sent to Canada to train new flyers. He proved to be a competent and popular instructor and was generous with his time in local communities. His arrival excited Fort Worth.

Castle was killed in a flying accident while teaching an American Signal Corps cadet. He was given a hero's funeral in Fort Worth, and his body was sent to New York where there was another huge funeral service and procession. He was buried in New York, with a dramatic statue of his wife Irene kneeling in grief by the grave. There is also a memorial to Vernon Castle in Fort Worth. An official Commonwealth War Graves Commission cemetery is also in Fort Worth, with graves of eleven IRFC cadets killed in training.

MY BELOVED HVSBAND
VERNON CASTLE BLYTH
BORN MAY 2, 1887
WAS KILLED FEB. 15, 1918
IN THE SERVICE OF HIS COVNTRY

CROIX DE GVERRE

Irene Castle mourned her hero husband with this touching memorial. The pair were played by Fred Astaire and Ginger Rogers in the classic film *The Story of Vernon and Irene Castle*. COURTESY NEIL FUNKHOUSER

Texas Fatality Rate

Learning to fly in the RFC in 1917 and 1918 was a dangerous activity. Gone were the sedate flights around Long Branch and the Curtiss Flying School. Cadets were encouraged to solo quickly and practise landings, takeoffs, loops, zooms, and other manoeuvres, extending their flight times and cross-country flying distances. Crashing in a slow JN-4 was not necessarily serious, and the machines, although flimsy, could often be easily repaired. But the fatality rate was an issue. In Toronto, the *Daily Star* newspaper carried out a campaign of criticism against the IRFC for its high accident and fatality rate. With more cadets under training, the number of fatalities rose over the winter in both Texas and Ontario.

When the IRFC left Texas, the *Austin American* newspaper reported that they would not be coming back. Among the reasons given was that it turned out that flying conditions were actually calmer in Ontario than in Texas. "The percentage of casualties to men who completed training in Fort Worth camps during March was 3.15 and the percentage of casualties to men in training in Canadian camps was 1.28."[4]

Among those killed in Texas was John Scott Rowan, twenty-three, of Nanaimo. Before joining the IRFC, he had attended Nanaimo High School and been a teacher near Powell River, BC. His parents were described as prominent citizens of Nanaimo. Rowan was one of two Canadian cadets killed in Texas on 29 March 1918. The announcement of his death in the *Nanaimo Free Press* on 30 March said he died while practising a spinning nose dive during a cross country test. His remains were returned to Nanaimo and his grave is in the Nanaimo public cemetery. It is unlikely he knew Osborne Orr, being behind him in training, although Rowan would have gone through Jesse Ketchum Induction Centre and No. 4 School of Military Aeronautics in Toronto at nearly the same time.

So, Orr may have been lucky to have stayed in Canada for his training that winter. Certainly, when the IRFC returned to Canada from Texas, a new training program was in place, with a special school established for instructors, and improved advance training being carried out at the new aerodrome in Beamsville, Ontario, near Niagara Falls. This was the School of Aerial Fighting. Despite the changes, learning to fly in 1918 remained a risky business.

Cadets Who Went On to Fame

While Vernon Castle was the big celebrity of the time in the IRFC, several of the young men who went through training had illustrious careers later. Roland Michener trained with the IRFC and later became Governor General of Canada. Mitchell Hepburn became the Premier of Ontario. Once the US entered the war in early 1917, US Army and Navy cadets were sent to be trained in Toronto or Texas. US Navy Cadet James Forrestal trained in Canada, and in the Second World War, was Secretary of the Navy and Secretary of Defence. Novelist William Faulkner was in training in Toronto with the RAF Canada when the war ended. He became a renowned American writer and winner of the Nobel Prize for Literature. It was found out that Faulkner often exaggerated his exploits in the RAF, but his notebooks have revealed the hard work required at No. 4 School of Military Aeronautics. Richard Arlen starred in *Wings*, the first motion picture to win an Academy Award. His performance may have had more authenticity than that of the other stars. Arlen joined the RFC in Canada and qualified as a pilot, but never saw combat.

Perhaps the most famous Canadian who served with the RAF Canada was another Nobel Prize winner—Lester "Mike" Pearson. In 1916, Pearson had dropped out of the University of Toronto and enlisted in the army medical corps. He served as a private at Salonika in northern Greece. He then transferred to the RAF and

Lester Bowles Pearson with the Canadian Army Medical Corps in Salonika, Greece. In the Royal Flying Corps, he became "Mike" Pearson. LIBRARY AND ARCHIVES CANADA / PA-117622

started training in England. There his name changed from Lester to Mike Pearson.

My Squadron Commander felt that Lester was no name for an aspiring fighter pilot and decided to call me Mike. It stuck and I was glad to lose Lester.[5]

Mike Pearson survived one training crash and was then severely injured when hit by a bus in the London blackout during a Zeppelin bombing attack. Invalided home to Canada in 1918, he was assigned to teach aerial navigation at No. 4 School of Military Aeronautics at the University of Toronto. Pearson was awarded the Noble Peace Prize in 1957 and was Prime Minister of Canada from 1963 to 1968.

Orr Stayed in Canada: Winter Training, 1917–18

Back in Canada, the winter of 1917–18 was severe, with trains stopped by snow and trucks unable to operate on the roads because of the –40-degree temperatures. Surprisingly, the flying training program was a success. Skis replaced landing wheels on the JN-4 Canucks. Mechanics adapted oil and coolants for the cold, and wire rigging on the wings was constantly checked for contraction and expansion. Perhaps the greatest challenge was protecting the pilots. When the JN-4 was cruising at 100 kilometres per hour, in temperatures of –20 degrees Celsius, the wind chill was fierce. With the pilots sitting in open cockpits, frostbite was common. At first Vaseline and whale oil were smeared on the face but proved inadequate. Face masks of chamois leather were effective. Nonetheless, winter flying in open unheated cockpits was chilling.

British ace James McCudden described the effect of flying in an open cockpit in winter. He was flying in an SE5 scout over France at higher altitudes than could be obtained in a Curtiss JN-4. But the

The winter of 1917–18 in Ontario was severe, but the Canadians in the IRFC proved winter flying could take place. Several types of skis were designed to keep the JN-4s flying. These are aircraft at Armour Heights in what is now Toronto. It is very possible that Cadet Orr is one of the men in the photo.

winter was colder in Ontario that year. The effect on the body would have been similar.

> I felt very ill indeed. This was not because of the height or the rapidity of my descent, but simply because of the intense cold which I experienced up high. The result was that when I got to lower altitude, and could breathe more oxygen, my heart beat more strongly and tried to force my sluggish and cold blood around my veins too quickly. The effect of this was to give me a feeling of faintness and exhaustion that can only be appreciated by those who have experienced it. My word, I did feel ill, and when I got on the ground and the blood returned to my veins, I can only describe the feeling as agony.[6]

The great Canadian ace Billy Bishop also described the impact of cold in a letter to his fiancée back in Canada dated 2 February 1916.

> This morning I went up for a three-and-a-half-hour patrol and it was the coldest I have ever seen here [France]. I got my right cheek badly frost bitten. It has swelled up and blistered and burst … it is extremely painful. I am spending the night in the hospital.[7]

The airmen of the IRFC who spent the winter of 1917–18 in extreme Ontario cold were pioneers in winter flying. In the three-month period from January to March 1918, the IRFC managed training flights on seventy-two days. The winter program was so successful that the IRFC did not intend to go to Texas again the next winter.

Osborne Orr learned to fly that winter. After a few hours flying with an instructor, it was IRFC policy to have cadets "go solo." Here there was great danger, and the number of crashes was frankly astonishing. Planes were regularly wrecked—there were dozens of accidents every day, as many as twenty-eight JN-4s were completely

Training at Armour Heights in Ontario in the winter of 1917–18. The cadet on the left seems to have frostbite. Osborne Orr would have trained in similar conditions. DIRECTORATE OF HISTORY AND HERITAGE, FONDS NO. 73/210, PHOTO ALBUM OF G.A. MACLEAN

destroyed in a month. Cadets often survived because the JN-4 was slow and just crumpled around them when they crashed. Still, the number of fatalities was quite high, with seven percent of cadets being killed in July 1917, and five percent in January 1918. Improved aircraft maintenance (the JN-4 had an unreliable engine that needed careful attention), new training methods, and better-trained instructors helped reduce the numbers, but the danger was real.

The IRFC and RAF Canada eventually trained more than 3,000 pilots and observers and 7,000 mechanics and aircraftsmen. Another 12,000 served in support. Fatalities were 137, with a further 39 Americans killed while training with the IRFC in Texas. It was a dangerous business.

As a Fighter Pilot, He "Made Good"

Osborne Orr passed through basic flight training at the Armour Heights aerodrome in North Toronto. Canadian Training Squadrons 91 and 92 were there at the time. He would have completed a machine gun course in Hamilton and then moved to Camp Borden near Barrie to practise cross country flying, artillery observation, and aerial fighting. Constant attention was paid to wireless, and the pilots were expected to master Morse code. On 9 March 1918, Orr graduated after 159 days with the Imperial Royal Flying Corps and became a second lieutenant in the Royal Flying Corps. He would have been granted leave and a last chance to see Virginia, then he sailed for England.

While he was on leave or even on the way to the UK, the Royal Flying Corps was amalgamated with the Royal Naval Air Service, and the Royal Air Force was created.

Orr's service record with the RAF in England starts on 25 April 1918. He was assigned to 45 Training Squadron and then to No. 1 Fighting School. He was learning to be a fighter pilot, flying the Camel.

Primitive by our standards, the Camel, built by the Sopwith company, was then a top-line fighter. Armed with two Vickers machine guns, it was a formidable airplane, and very hard to fly. According to aviation historian Robert Jackson, "In the hands of a novice it displayed vicious characteristics that could make it a killer; but under the firm touch of a skilled pilot, who knew how to turn its vices to his own advantage, it was one of the most superb fighting machines ever built."[8]

In all, 385 men died in training, learning to fly Camels.

When Orr qualified, he was posted to 204 Squadron. Until the 1 April formation of the RAF, this squadron had been No. 4 Squadron of the Royal Naval Air Service, and some of its pilots still wore their naval uniforms. Having been the among the first squadrons to fly the Camel in 1917, they were an experienced group. The fact that he

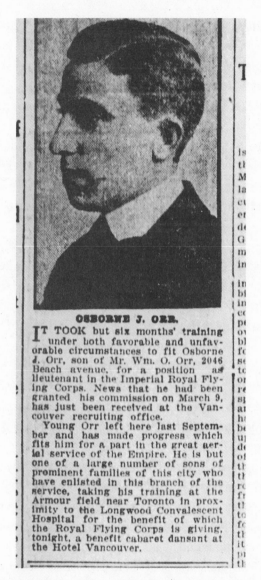

OSBORNE J. ORR.

IT TOOK but six months' training under both favorable and unfavorable circumstances to fit Osborne J. Orr, son of Mr. Wm. O. Orr, 2046 Beach avenue, for a position as lieutenant in the Imperial Royal Flying Corps. News that he had been granted his commission on March 9, has just been received at the Vancouver recruiting office.

Young Orr left here last September and has made progress which fits him for a part in the great aerial service of the Empire. He is but one of a large number of sons of prominent families of this city who have enlisted in this branch of the service, taking his training at the Armour field near Toronto in proximity to the Longwood Convalescent Hospital for the benefit of which the Royal Flying Corps is giving, tonight, a benefit cabaret dansant at the Hotel Vancouver.

Lieut. Orr's proud parents made sure that his commission was announced in the Vancouver *Province* newspaper. They seem to think he had "made good." There is no mention of Virginia. THE DAILY PROVINCE, VANCOUVER, 22 MARCH 1918. PAGE 19. A DIVISION OF POSTMEDIA NETWORK, INC.

joined 204 has created some confusion and some historical accounts place Orr in the RNAS. As we have seen he was always RFC/RAF.

Nearly half of the pilots in 204 Squadron were also Canadians, making Orr's integration into the experienced group somewhat easier. Some, at least of the ground crew, would have remembered Sidney Ellis, killed the previous summer stunting in his Camel (see Part 1, page 62). The most successful pilot in the squadron was C.R.R. Hickey, who shot down twenty-one enemy aircraft.

Charlie Hickey—Another Ace from Nanaimo

By chance—perhaps by pleasant chance for Orr—Hickey was from Nanaimo. Charles Robert Reeves Hickey was born in Nanaimo in 1897, making him just twenty-one years old when Orr arrived at 204 Squadron, but Charlie was senior to Orr in experience in the air, in success as a fighter pilot, and in rank. Charlie was brought up in Parksville, just a few kilometres north of Nanaimo, and he attended Nanaimo High School. His father, Major Robert Hume Fryer Hickey, had given up his career in the British Army to become a rancher near French Creek, between Parksville and Qualicum Beach. This is a surprising occupation title, for the area is a heavily treed rainforest. His mother was Charlotte Reeves Hickey.

At age eighteen, Charlie joined the Canadian Army in Victoria, BC, on 17 March 1916 and went overseas with the Canadian Mounted Rifles. Charlie spent the next nine months training in a reserve battalion in England. He transferred, perhaps with his father's connections and help, to the Royal Naval Air Service in January 1917. The final entry in his Canadian Army record said he was "honest, sober, trustworthy, and intelligent."

Hickey completed training in July 1917, with his highest marks (82 per cent) in Navigation and Gunnery. He was recommended for scouts, his report deeming him a "Good officer and pilot." He was posted to 4 Naval Air Squadron, and by the time the RNAS and RFC

Charlie Hickey, one of the young aces from Vancouver Island—he was just twenty years old when he posed in his naval uniform. COURTESY PARKSVILLE MUSEUM ARCHIVES

were merged in April 1918, he had four victories and was characterized in reports as "a good fighting pilot, good command of men."

Hickey became an ace in April 1918 but was burned in a strange accident. On 21 April he forced down a German Rumpler C machine and then landed beside it. Many pilots did this to get souvenirs. He was trying to protect his prize from Belgian civilians when it exploded, killing several bystanders and burning Hickey on the face and hands.

By the time Orr arrived at 204 Squadron, Hickey was a captain and had scored nine victories. He added twelve more after Orr arrived.

Orr in Combat—Unrelenting Danger and Stress

Feeling at home with Hickey may have contributed to Orr's successes. He was soon in the thick of the fighting and on 12 August he shot down two German Fokker D.VIIs. The D.VII could climb faster than the Camel and had a higher top speed. It was considered by some to be the best fighter of the war. However, the Camel was agile and could turn quickly, so Orr had quickly proved his skills and determination.

On 13 August, 204 Squadron combined with 210, 213, and 17th United States Aero Squadron for an attack by fifty Camel fighters on the German airbase at Varssenaere. Describing the attack in the official history, S.F. Wise wrote, "On the ground there was chaos, the Germans having been caught with flights of Fokkers lined up for takeoff." Flying as low as five metres, the Camels machine-gunned and bombed the aircraft, hangars, and barracks.

On 15 August, 204 Squadron was again in the thick of things. In the morning they fought thirteen Fokkers near Ypres and shot down four, with two of these claimed by Lieutenant W.B. Craig of Smiths Falls, Ontario. That evening, 204 flew again and fought a fifteen-minute battle with a large German formation. Captain Hickey shot down one of them.

Osborne Orr shot down a D.VII on 14 August and another one the day after that. Four superior German aircraft shot down in four days—Orr was a good pilot and a good shot.

These victories were scored in the sky over one of the greatest battles of the war. On 8 August, the Canadian Corps and the Australian Corps of the British Army had launched an attack that broke the German Army. The Canadians and Australians defeated the Germans in battle after battle—Amiens, Arras, Canal du Nord, Mons—while in the sky, the RAF fought big battles against the German air force. Camel squadrons also bombed and strafed German trenches and scouted ahead of tanks, looking for and destroying anti-tank guns. In a hundred days, the war would be over.

For the next two months, Orr and 204 Squadron were in constant action. For example, on 16 September nineteen Camels from 204 Squadron fought with nineteen Fokkers and seven other German aircraft over Ostend and Blankenberge. Hickey and two others scored victories in this aerial melee. Then Hickey and another pilot from 204—a Lieutenant Mathey—were killed on 3 October when their aircraft collided while diving through clouds.

The intensity of operations wore down the young pilots, and in fact years later many talked about the constant fatigue they experienced. In Part One we saw how this unrelenting physical and mental stress wore down pilots such as Playford Hales. These great battles produced heavy casualties. In August, the RAF lost 215 machines, the highest monthly loss of the war. In September, 235 machines were lost. In October, another 164.

Then on 14 October, Orr shot down his fifth German aircraft, an LVG reconnaissance plane. He was now an ace. We can imagine that, despite the tiring pace of operations, there might have been a celebration in the squadron mess, as the young men defied the odds and toasted success.

More from "Ace Island"—Collishaw and Fall

If the RAF was an elite force, then the aces were the elite of the elite. Shooting down five enemy aircraft was not something easily done. Most air battles were true melees. Both planes in a dogfight were moving—twisting, diving, looping. Hitting another with machine gun fire was hard, and doing it consistently was very hard indeed. The scores accredited to the top aces are really astounding. The pilots of the First World War were the height of glamour because flying was new, adventurous, and dangerous. The aces topped that.

The website for the Aerodrome[9] has a list of all of the aces on both sides in the First World War. There were just 1,865. With five victories, Osborne Orr ranks with 313 other flyers at the end of the list. There were 194 Canadian aces. The Aerodrome's top ten aces are:

1. Manfred von Richthofen, Germany, 80

2. Rene Fonck, France, 75

3. William "Billy" Bishop, Canada, 72

4. Ernst Udet, Germany, 62

5. Edward Mannock, UK, 61

6. Raymond Collishaw, Canada, 60

7. James McCudden, UK, 57

8. Andrew Beauchamp-Proctor, UK, 54

9. Erich Lowenhardt, Germany, 54

10. Donald MacLaren, Canada, 54

Osborne Orr and Charlie Hickey had something in common with Canada's second-highest-scoring ace, Raymond Collishaw. They were all born in Nanaimo, British Columbia. Collishaw was born there in 1893. Did they know each other as little boys? There is no evidence. Did Orr or Hickey in 204 Squadron ever meet Collishaw in 203 Squadron? We can only speculate.

Collishaw is of course the most famous of these Vancouver Island aces. He stayed in the RAF after the war and served in Russia as a squadron commander when the Allies intervened in the Russian revolution. By 1939, Collishaw was the senior operational commander of the RAF in Egypt and the Western Desert of North Africa. He retired from the RAF as an air vice-marshal and returned to Vancouver, dying there in 1976. In a 1969 CBC interview, Collishaw said of air combat, "It was straight forward dueling. The luckiest man won. It was more luck than it was anything else."

Another ace from Vancouver Island was Joseph Fall, who was from Cobble Hill, a village near the city of Duncan. This is sixty-five kilometres south of Nanaimo, and it is unlikely that Fall would know the men from Nanaimo. What he had in common with Collishaw and Hickey was the Royal Naval Air Service.

In a speech to the Canadian Museum of Flight in 1988, his son described Fall's career. Born in 1895, the same year as Orr, he grew up on a farm and attended Cowichan Public School and Quamichan Lake Private School, which prepared boys for the Royal Military College of Canada. In 1915 he tried to join the army but was rejected on medical grounds. He had suffered a severe head injury in a farm accident. Fall was nothing if not determined, so he took lessons at Stinson School of Flying in Dayton, Ohio. He then signed up to take flying lessons in Montreal, but the school's only plane crashed. Fall then paid his own way to England and applied to the Royal Naval Air Service. "When they asked me if I had any bodily injuries, I said no. They didn't ask me anything about head injuries and I didn't offer anything." He was accepted, probably on the basis of his flying instruction in Ohio.

Raymond Collishaw of Nanaimo was commander of 203 Squadron, RAF, 12 July 1918. He is standing centre, still wearing his RNAS uniform. The Camel fighters lined up behind the pilots were difficult to fly, but deadly in the hands of skilled pilots. CANADA DEPARTMENT OF NATIONAL DEFENCE / LIBRARY AND ARCHIVES CANADA / PA-002792

Another great ace from Vancouver Island. Joseph Fall stands beside his scout. He survived the war. His family still lives on Vancouver Island. COURTESY FALL FAMILY COLLECTION

Fall finished his training in October 1916 and was assigned to 3 Naval Squadron in France. Nine of the twelve pilots were Canadians, and one of them was Raymond Collishaw. Fall was in the air over Vimy Ridge during the great battle there in April 1917 and had three victories on 11 April. He became an ace later that month—before Collishaw was. By the end of 1917, Joseph Fall had shot down thirty-six aircraft and two balloons. He became the only pilot in history to be awarded the Distinguished Service Cross three times.

An exhausted Joe Fall was granted home leave, and when he returned from Canada in April 1918 was assigned to the School of Aerial Fighting at Frieston in England. He was an instructor for the rest of the war. For this he was awarded the Air Force Cross, a medal reserved for distinguished service in non-combat roles. At the end of the war, Fall remained in the RAF and flew from early aircraft carriers, was a test pilot, and served in the Middle East. During the Second World War, he commanded RAF stations in Malta and

Egypt, then No. 33 Elementary Flying Training School in Carberry, Manitoba. In 1945, Fall retired from the RAF and returned to the farm in Cobble Hill, BC, where he raised champion Jersey cows. He died in Duncan, BC, in 1988, age 93.

It is remarkable that Fall, Orr, Collishaw, and Hickey were all born on Vancouver Island within a few kilometres of each other. Oddly, for reasons now unknown, Orr is not listed among the Canadians in 204 Squadron by S.F. Wise in the official history, *Canadian Airmen and the First World War*.

Missing in Action

Now we return to the misty morning of 23 October in Northern France, when 204 Squadron was to take part in a bombing mission. The fighter pilots dropped 12-kilogram bombs and used their machine guns on ground targets, while protecting other bombers. The aggressive Camel pilots (all of them surely) would be on the lookout for a chance to score. On the return flight, they ran into enemy fighters near Termonde in eastern Belgium. In the melee that developed, 204 Squadron and Osborne Orr ran out of luck. Four Camels were shot down. Orr was missing in action.

News of casualties was delivered by a telegram. Virginia was listed on Orr's record as his next of kin, so the dreaded official notice that he was missing in action would go to her. Virginia was twenty years old and a widow. She was still living in Toronto and living on Osborne's RAF pay.

Orr's parents contacted newspapers, including the *Vancouver Daily World* on 8 November. On 12 December, the *Daily World* reported, "No further word has been received by his relatives... his mother and his sister who reside at 1676 Pendrill St., believe there may be a possibility that he will still turn up. It is thought that his machine was injured in his last flight because he was seen to dive from a great height but so far no trace has been found of his machine or himself." They did not mention Virginia, again.

Widow

For twenty-year-old Virginia Orr, the pain must have been immense. She was alone in Toronto, without her family in Spokane or her in-laws in Vancouver. She would get letters from the 204 Squadron Leader and from other pilots. Eventually personal effects made their way back. With the war over on 11 November, the RAF was able to search for Osborne's body. It was never found.

His name is listed on the Arras Flying Services Memorial in France, which commemorates almost a thousand airmen of the Royal Naval Air Service, the Royal Flying Corps, the Australian Flying Corps, and the Royal Air Force who were killed on the Western Front and have no known grave.

On 1 January 1919, the King's New Year's Honours List named Orr as recipient of the Distinguished Flying Cross. This medal would have been sent to Virginia with Osborne's name engraved on the back. The DFC was awarded for bravery in action against the enemy and was also recognition of Orr's status as an ace.

This precious medal was rediscovered in 2021 in Seattle by Constance Jill Thayer and her brother James Stewart Thayer amongst items in their brother's estate. It had passed from Virginia Orr into the hands of Caroline Orr, and then on down the generations. The Thayers wanted to see it repatriated and generously donated the DFC, and other medals and papers, to the Vancouver Island Military Museum.

Virginia would later also receive the bronze Next of Kin Memorial Plaque and a scroll with a message from the King. The wording of the scroll was:

MASON C. J.
MELLOR D. J. T.
MILLAR K. O.
MISENER M. S.
MOIR C. J.
MOORE R.
MULROY H. J.
NELSON H. L.
NICHOLSON O. H.
NICOLSON J.
NIELSEN P.
NOEL H. C.
NUNN F. A. W.
ORR O. J. D. F. C.
O'SHEA H. A.
OWEN W. T.
PAYNE S. T.
PAYTON J. L.
PELL W. A.
PIERCE J. B.
PIM T.
PRIDEAUX E. R.
RAMSAY G. S.
REID J. C. M.

The Arras Flying Services Memorial in France lists the names of 984 flyers with no known grave. COURTESY LADY LINDA, FINDAGRAVE.COM

He whom this scroll commemorates
was numbered among those who,
at the call of King and country, left all
that was dear to them, endured hardness,
faced danger, and finally passed out of
the sight of men by the path of duty
and self-sacrifice, giving up their own
lives that others might live in freedom.
Let those who come after see to it
that his name be not forgotten.
2nd Lt. Osborne John Orr
Royal Air Force

The plaque was often called "Dead Man's Penny" though eleven centimetres in diameter and bronze. Over one million were issued, and many have survived, but so far, not Orr's.

Orr's parents had his name added to the war memorial at St. Paul's Anglican Church in Vancouver, along with the names of fifty-two other parishioners killed in the war. The names are listed under two inscriptions:

FOR GOD, KING, AND COUNTRY

THEY CLIMBED THE STEEP ASCENT TO
HEAVEN IN PERIL, TOIL, AND PAIN

At Britannia High School, a war memorial was unveiled at a ceremony in 1921. It consisted of three carved wooden panels—one for staff who served, one for students who served, and one for those who died. Orr and another man were not there. The principal, Mr. Dunning, noted in his dedication speech that the two missing names would be added later.

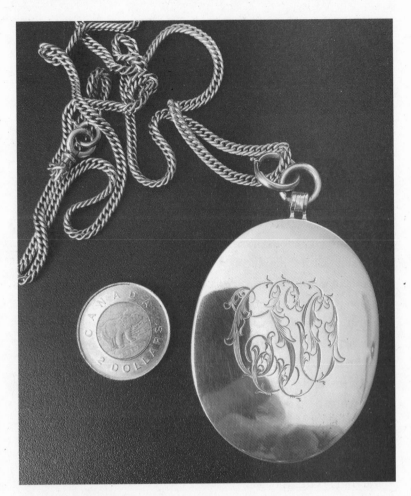

The locket. Caroline Orr wore it for the rest of her life. It is a precious memento today for her relatives in Seattle. COURTESY JAMES THAYER

The Locket

The proud mother who had sent her troubled son ten dollars to see him through was clearly devastated. Caroline Orr wore the portrait of her son around her neck for the rest of her life. In the picture, he is wearing the ribbon of the Distinguished Flying Cross which he never got to wear in life. Mounted in a beautiful silver locket with Caroline's initial on the cover, it has survived for over a century and is a moving and personal memorial to a young man who had experienced some troubles as a teen but had become an officer and decorated hero.

The Gratuity Issue

Virginia Orr faced a potentially difficult future. Married women were not expected to work outside the home, but how would she and hundreds of thousands of other widows survive? Governments had to deal with that issue as well as how to care for the hundreds of thousands of veterans who were wounded in body and mind. Virginia received a British government gratuity and a pension. The gratuity was a lump sum payment based on rank and length of service. The widow of a temporary second lieutenant received a pension of £120 per year (£2.30 weekly). At our distance from the war, it is difficult to make a monetary comparison. This would have been about $600 per year, at a time when a new Ford Model T was $400, a pound of butter cost 63 cents, and roast beef was 39 cents per pound.

Pensions for widows and war wounded became a great issue immediately after the war.

In 1919, tens of thousands of soldiers returned to Canada each month and were demobilized—left the army. The Canadian government had made provision of pensions, and medical care of the wounded veterans. The War Service Gratuity was a one-time payment to help returned men adjust to civilian life. The amount was based on rank and length of service. A married private who had served overseas for three years would get $600.

But many veterans found it difficult to return to civilian life and most were shocked at the cost of living and at the wealth around

English Bay, 1916. Beach Ave. Ferguson Pt. Englesea Lodge; English Bay Pier, demolished 1930; Sylvia Court. Alexandra Park. Here John Morton landed 1862 City Archives

Englesea Lodge (left of centre) at the entrance to Stanley Park, 1916. Virginia Orr lived here in 1920. Her relationship with the Orr family remains a mystery.

them. Those who stayed at home during the war had good jobs and made much more money than the troops. A soldier's pay had not been raised during the war, but inflation was rampant at home, and many soldiers found their family leading a threadbare life. Jobs were scarce, and discontent grew throughout 1919. A veterans' movement soon demanded an additional bonus payment of $2,000. To the government this seemed a shocking amount on top or the War Service Gratuity—it could cost a billion dollars. Historian Desmond Morton summarized the veterans' position.

> A gratuity of $2000 seemed little enough thanks from affluent fellow-citizens. If the war had dragged on for a further year, Canadians would have paid far more. Such a bonus would be big enough to solve any man's re-establishment problem.[10]

In the face of public demonstrations and widespread agitation, in November 1919 the government made some limited concessions to the veterans' bonus movement. The War Service Gratuity was extended to those who had served in the RAF, and there would be a $25 million winter relief program for veterans.

By January 1920, Mrs. Virginia Orr had moved back to Vancouver and was living at the Englesea Lodge Apartments on Beach Drive in Vancouver. She applied to the Canadian government for the now available Canadian War Service Gratuity. The application has survived in the archives in Ottawa.

Virginia's application was denied. One of the regulations for the dispersal of the money was that the veteran had to have been a resident of Canada when the war started on 4 August 1914. Although a Canadian, Osborne was a resident of St. Paul, Minnesota, on that date.

The veterans' bonus campaign failed as well.

Virginia Orr moved permanently to the United States shortly after losing her application for the gratuity. Her mother and brother Proctor Kennedy lived in Seattle. She had relatives in Los Angeles.

The 1940 US Census places her in San Francisco and describes her as a widow and a manicurist. With a job and her pensions, she was surviving. In 1952 in Carson, Nevada, she married a man named H.O. Stumbaugh. She died in 1973 and is buried in Seattle, alongside her mother "Nettie" Kennedy and near her brother Proctor M. Kennedy.

A Hero Rediscovered

In November 2019, Allan Snowie visited the Nanaimo Cenotaph and hoped to see there the name of local hero Osborne Orr. Allan is a retired Royal Canadian Navy pilot and Air Canada pilot who has written several books on Canadian military topics. Allan wondered why a local hero would not be on the cenotaph. He had written briefly about Osborne Orr and had found his Nanaimo birth certificate. Snowie is also a friend of the Vancouver Island Military Museum and contacted them about having Orr's name added to the Nanaimo Cenotaph. He donated five hundred dollars to have a plaque made. The museum investigated, and this author wrote up initial findings in the *VIMM Newsletter*. Museum President Roger Bird then made arrangements with the City of Nanaimo to have Orr's name added at the 2020 Remembrance Day ceremony at the cenotaph.

Investigating how Orr is remembered reveals some of the problems created in our internet age. The website Canada's Virtual War Memorial[11] lists Orr correctly and has a photo of Orr, supplied by James Thayer of Seattle. Unlike many websites, they do have his birthplace correct, as does the Commonwealth War Graves Commission. The Aerodrome website has good and accurate information about Orr as well. But there is a widespread claim, site after site across the internet, that Orr was an American who joined the RFC. He is often listed as an American ace. There is even a photo of a man mistakenly identified as Orr, wearing a uniform that is totally

HINDS. J. T.	102 ND		THOMSON. ROBERT G. 16 TH
HOGGAN, DAVID	29 TH		THORNE. W. E. H.	7 TH
HONEYMAN. ROBERT	13 TH G.F.AMBULANCE		WADDINGTON WILLIAM I.10 T.H
JACK. GEORGE	2 ND C. M. R.		WAKELEM. THOMAS
JACKSON. THOMAS	75 TH BATTALION		WARN. LANCE	16 TH
JEPSON. H. R.	47 TH		WATSON. JAMES H.	47 TH
JEPSON. J. A.	29 TH		WATSON. JOHN	29 TH
JOHNSTON. DUNCAN	72 ND		WATSON. J. W.
JONES. EDMUND T.	31 ST		WICKING-SMITH. B. J.
JURIET. WILLIAM F.	29 TH		WILLIAMSON. A.
KNOX. JOHN	4 TH		WILSON. CARL C. H. M. S. NIOBE
LANGLANDS. J. A.	56 TH		WILSON. RUPERT L. 7 TH BATTALION
LUCAS. JOHN	13 TH C.F.AMBULANCE		WILKINSON. JOHN 11 TH C. M. R.
MALPASS. ARNOLD V.	7 TH BATTALION		YOUNG. JOHN H. M.S. GALLIANO

THEIR NAMES SHALL LIVE FOR EVERMORE

ORR, OSBORNE J. RFC/RAF

Orr's name added to the Nanaimo Cenotaph. A. SCULLY

incorrect, and clearly from the nineteenth century. Many internet sources also incorrectly place Orr in the Royal Naval Air Service.

The origin of the claim that Orr was an American ace serving in the RAF lies in a book that has been accepted as a "prime source" of information about aces. *Above the Trenches* by Christopher Shores, Norman Franks, and Russell Guest is a wonder of compilation; however, errors can be normally expected in such a massive undertaking. In addition, it was written before the digital age that has made ready access to archives. Shores, Franks, and Guest state that Orr was born in Ohio. The evidence about his background is clear and now readily available. His residence in St. Paul is hard to discover and seems unlikely to have been the cause of the error. The real reason for the error may be a misreading of his marriage licence, where Virginia Kennedy's birthplace in Ohio is listed. Sadly, once an error is on the internet, it is almost impossible to correct and is constantly repeated. It is important to get original documents.

We have seen that Orr was never in the RNAS. But he did join RAF 204 Squadron, which had been Naval 4. Again, a simple error changed the story of Orr's life.

The photo of Orr on Canada's Virtual War Memorial led to the discovery of the wonderful artifacts in the possession of the Thayer family of Seattle. James Thayer granted me permission to use the photo in a story about Orr in the newsletter of the Vancouver Island Military Museum. A continuing correspondence with Jim revealed that through his mother's family, he was related to the Stewart family in Nanaimo, made regular visits there, and was in possession of a wealth of material that connected to Orr. We exchanged research and the locket came to light. It is an emotionally important artifact, linking the story of an air warrior to a mother's grief.

When Orr's name was added to the Nanaimo Cenotaph in 1920, neither Jim Thayer nor Allan Snowie was able to attend because of COVID-19 pandemic restrictions. Jim was also anxious to see the VIMM display on Orr that was installed in the spring of 2021, but again pandemic restrictions intervened. His photo of the locket plays a central part in that display, as do his photos of the Stewart family of Nanaimo, and Orr in civilian clothes.

In January of 2021, Jim and his sister Connie Thayer made an astonishing discovery. In the effects of the estate of their recently deceased brother they found a treasure trove of artifacts related to Orr. There, in original, untouched condition, in its original box, was Orr's DFC. There also were his RFC wings, awarded in Toronto just weeks before the RFC became the RAF. The find included Orr's service medals and the documentation sent with the medals. The solid silver DFC is engraved with his name and rank, his date of death, and his squadron. The DFC ribbon is the original. This discovery is quite amazing but was followed by a generous act. Jim and Connie offered to repatriate these items to Canada, in the care of the Vancouver Island Military Museum. They are a precious addition to the museum.

Orr's Distinguished Flying Cross, found in 2021. A. SCULLY

How these items ended up with the family of Caroline Stewart Orr and not with Virginia Orr remains a mystery.

"Bring Our Boys Back Home"

Perhaps the most important memorial to Osborne Orr takes place at the high school he attended. Britannia Secondary School is now the oldest high school in Vancouver. Every year on Remembrance Day, the school honours the eighteen Britannia students who fought and died overseas by holding up placards with the names of each young man. Teacher Sarah Diane Ng organized the ceremony from 2000 to 2017. "Our intention," says Ng, "was to bring our boys back home through intentional acts of remembering. Osborne Orr was one of the Britannia students we honoured every year." In this way thousands of young Canadian, annually remember Osborne. He is neither obscure nor forgotten. He is an ace and he "made good."

3

YOUTH TRANSCENDED

MAKING A FLYING WORLD

Though the Jazz Age continues it became less
and less an affair of youth. The sequel was
like a children's party taken over by the elders.

F. SCOTT FITZGERALD
Commenting on the
year 1922 in *Echoes of the Jazz Age*

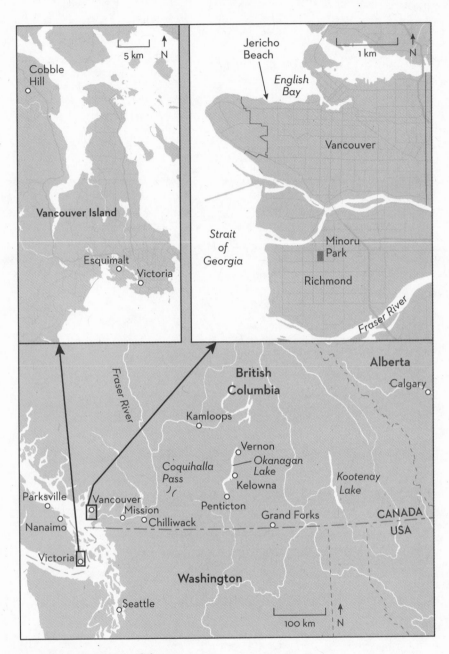

Western Canada and the US.

THE REMARKABLE PHOTO on the next page captures a moment in the lives of two young Canadian pilots who were flying instructors at the School of Aerial Fighting in Beamsville, Ontario, in 1918. At twenty-eight, Captain Godfrey is a Royal Air Force fighter ace and commander of the school. Lieutenant Trim has not seen aerial combat but, at twenty-three, is a veteran pilot and soldier. They are standing next to a Curtiss JN-4 (Can) training aircraft, painted to look like a German fighter.[1]

Godfrey looks every inch the ace pilot of the First World War—the riding breeches, and that scarf. Classic. Is that the steely eyed look of a deadly fighter pilot? Trim is dressed in a bulky leather shearling coat with the now iconic pilot's leather helmet with goggles. He needed that outfit to keep warm at higher altitudes and especially in the open, unheated cockpit of the Curtiss machine. It may only have flown at a speed of 120 kilometres per hour but at 3,000 metres

altitude, the temperature was about –5 degrees Celsius, and the wind chill was nasty. Both men played important roles in Canadian aviation history.

Godfrey needs no introduction to many people. He was a fighter ace. He is a member of the Canadian Aviation Hall of Fame and winner of the prestigious McKee Trophy, an award given annually for contribution to the advancement of Canadian aviation. Godfrey was also an air vice-marshal in the Royal Canadian Air Force in the Second World War.

Trim is basically unknown today but played an important role in early aviation in British Columbia and Quebec. He has been briefly mentioned in one or two histories of aviation but assigned to the role of second fiddle to the accomplishments of others. But the story behind the photo tells us that, within a year of this photo, he was constantly in the news—flying Hollywood stars, racing against cars, shaking hands with the Prince of Wales, making daring flights into the interior of BC, setting records, surviving crashes, and entertaining thousands who were seeing their first airplane. Trim was having fun. Within another year, he became the managing director of an airline—one of the first in Canada. Then his airline was ruined. He joined the brand-new Royal Canadian Air Force and later moved to Quebec, where he became a safety expert. In 1940, he engaged in a daring rescue attempt in remote Labrador and testified as an expert witness in a then famous, but now forgotten, trial. He was far more than a second fiddle.

When the war ended, both flyers ended up in Vancouver, but in very different capacities. Perhaps the photo shows a bit of that difference. Godfrey, the base commander, looks "dashing" but stern. He is a commander. Trim, younger and fresh faced, perhaps looks a little cheeky. In Vancouver, they would both be associated with another famous airman, ace, and future member of the Canadian Aviation Hall of Fame, Donald MacLaren. These three and other veterans of the Royal Flying Corps and Royal Air Force were founders of civilian aviation in British Columbia and Canada. Trim and Godfrey were also among the few pilots who were in the Royal Canadian Air Force when it was created in 1924. When we look at this remarkable photo today, we are looking into the past, and in exploring their lives, we are able to discover an exciting, glamorous, and dangerous time in our history.

The Temperament of Successful Aviators

The history of Godfrey and Trim is based on research in publicly available documents. Insights into their character and personality are difficult, especially for George Trim, who after 1920 lived a more private life than Godfrey. Trim did not leave any diaries or letters to provide insight into the man. There is more known about Godfrey because of his famous career. For that reason, this history pays more attention to trying to reveal something about the lesser-known George Trim.

They had in common their service during the Great War in the Royal Flying Corps and Royal Air Force. Those organizations had very clear ideas about the types of young men that it wanted for pilot training. When there was a shortage of recruits, these characteristics might not all be met, but we can today get an idea of what kinds of young men we are dealing with.

The Lancet, probably then, and now, the foremost medical journal in the world, published an article in September 1918 by two RAF officers. They discussed the characteristics wanted in a pilot.[2]

> He possesses resolution, initiative, presence of mind, sense of humour, judgement; is alert, cheerful, optimistic, happy-go-lucky, generally a good fellow, and frequently lacking in imagination.

Anyone who has lived with pilots for any length of time cannot fail to notice that they possess in a very high degree a fund of animal spirits and excessive vitality.

When they have finished flying for the day their favourite amusements are theatres, music (chiefly ragtime), cards, and dancing, and it appears necessary for the well-being of the average pilot that he indulge in a really riotous evening at least once or twice a month.

One of the most important characteristics we have noticed in successful aviators is, "hands." The pilot with good hands senses unconsciously the various movements of the aeroplane and rectifies any unusual or abnormal evolutions almost before they occur. He is invariably a graceful flyer, never unconsciously throws an undue strain on the machine . . .

The fighting scout is usually the enthusiastic youngster, keen of flying, full of what one might call the "joy of life," possessing an average intelligence. He has little or no imagination, no sense of responsibility, keen sense of humour, able to think and act quickly.

While this list of characteristics described in a medical journal in 1918 should not be used to judge all aviators, then or now, it gives us some insight into what many pilots in the First World War might have been like. Surely, some of these characteristics fit the students at the Curtiss Flying School in 1916 and Osborne Orr.

George Knopp Trim

George Trim was born in England in 1895, the same year as Osborne Orr. His attestation papers, completed when he joined the Canadian Army at Camp Valcartier Quebec on 23 September 1914, gave his mother's address as Vancouver, but he had been working as a bank clerk in Battleford, Saskatchewan. He was five foot seven and weighed 152 pounds, with grey eyes and fair hair. He went overseas

Oxford School of Military Aeronautics class learning airframe rigging. This photo might be confused with one taken in Toronto at the same time. IMPERIAL WAR MUSEUM Q27250

with the 10th Battalion in October 1914. The army moves in mysterious ways, and Trim's record shows that he was soon posted to a variety of desk jobs in England with the army's records office. He was quickly made a sergeant, and at the end of May 1915, he was promoted to staff sergeant at the age of twenty. This is a responsible and important administrative rank among non-commissioned officers. Trim was then transferred to the staff of the Canadian Convalescent Depot (CCD) in Bath, England. He must have made a very good impression, for he was promoted again to company sergeant major (CSM) at the age of twenty-one.[3]

To become a CSM at such a young age certainly tells us something about Trim. The image of a sergeant major is one of a burly, tough, red-faced soldier shouting orders. Certainly, it was a respected rank, with a great deal of responsibility and even power. A sergeant major was a warrant officer and superior to all non-commissioned officers. Commissioned officers were superior, but it was a foolish junior officer—a lieutenant—who did not listen to a sergeant major's suggestions and comments. A CSM supervised all the sergeants in his company, strictly overseeing the performance of their duties. Reporting to the officer commanding a company (in Trim's case probably the commander of the CCD), the CSM was responsible for discipline and day-to-day supervision of the soldiers. Trim was not likely to have done a lot of shouting on a parade square.

Evidently Trim was not happy with his desk job, and he transferred to the Royal Flying Corps in April 1917.[4] Flying itself was dangerous and fighting the German air force was a deadly business. Trim wanted to be in the fight, and he left the safety of an administrative position for the excitement, glamour, and danger of flying.[5]

Trim's flying career began as a cadet in England at Denham for basic training.[6] An English cadet described his experience at Denham as "a sort of hades composed of mud, weather-board sheds, and red-faced sergeants—a hideous phantasma. Another month of it would have pretty well broken me up."[7] The experience might have only been somewhat annoying for Company Sergeant Major Trim. He may have been a cadet, and he may have been young, but he had been a sergeant major, and few people trifled with a sergeant major. He then went to No. 2 School of Military Aeronautics operating at Oxford University.

The RFC had high standards of education, on paper at least, and expected cadets to come into the service with very good skills in mathematics. It is worth revisiting the RFC description of an ideal cadet.

Ideally, he should be between eighteen and twenty-five years of age, have matriculated from high school, and have spent a couple of years at university. He should be well grounded in algebra and geometry, be able to 'speak the King's English,' and bear 'the earmarks of a gentleman.' . . . the type of fellow wanted as a pilot . . . is the clean bred chap with lots of the devil in him.[8]

In Britain's class-conscious society, an officer was expected to be a gentleman and have a gentleman's education. The RFC perpetuated that image in its recruiting posters. Men like George Trim and Earl Godfrey, sergeants from the "colonies," were, under normal peacetime conditions, unlikely to have been accepted as officers. But the reality was that pilots were desperately needed.

At Oxford, Trim took classroom courses similar to those at No. 4 School of Military Aeronautics at the University of Toronto. Discipline was relaxed, but the courses were eight hours a day, six day a week, with constant testing and final examinations. Those without the background or drive to master the theory of war flying were weeded out. Successful cadets graduated to flight training.

Cadet Trim then went to Training Squadrons 41 and 43 to actually learn to fly. Crashes were frequent and treated as normal. Many cadets were injured or killed in flight training, but Trim was successful as a pilot. His record also states that he was "a first class shot." But ill health plagued Trim throughout 1917. He had been hospitalized for rheumatism in the Canadian Army but returned fit for duty.[9] That condition may have returned. Whatever ailed Trim, he was grounded as unfit for flying for five months.[10] When he was healthy again, he was assigned to training cadets, a job often given to good student pilots, much to the disappointment of most.

A good pilot and a good shot but plagued with illness. This made Trim a candidate for assignment back to Canada, to the Royal Air Force Canada as an instructor. When Lieutenant Trim arrived at the School of Aerial Gunnery in Beamsville, Ontario, in May 1918, his RAF record showed that he had experience flying five types of aircraft, including the Sopwith Pup, which was a scout. In Toronto he was hospitalized again almost immediately. Bad luck and bad health.

Albert Earl Godfrey

Godfrey was born in Killarney, Manitoba, in 1890 and lived in Vancouver and Seattle before he joined the army in 1915. His Canadian attestation papers state that he was a gunsmith, but his RAF service record lists him as a mechanical engineer. He was also a well-known motorcycle racer in Vancouver and Seattle and considered "daring." In 1911, at Minoru Park near Vancouver, Godfrey won a five-mile race in seven minutes and nine seconds on his four-horsepower Excelsior bike.[11] Godfrey was also in the news as a marksman. He was a private in Vancouver's Sixth Regiment, the Duke of Connaught's Own Rifles, when he was awarded a Marksman Badge (Class 1) at the annual regimental shoot in December 1910.[11] When he joined the army in Winnipeg in 1915, he was five foot eight and 160 pounds, with blue eyes and fair hair.

Godfrey's battalion went to France in March 1916, attached to the First Canadian Division. In May, at the age of twenty-six, he was promoted to armourer sergeant, and he would have been an expert in the repair and maintenance of rifles, pistols, and machine guns. The pioneers often served in, or just behind, the trenches at the front and theirs was certainly not a safe job, although not as dangerous as the infantry.

In August 1916, Godfrey transferred to the RFC. He first trained as an observer, and joined 25 Squadron, RFC. An observer did just that, usually spotting for the artillery. Guiding the fire of the artillery below was one of the most important roles of the RFC, perhaps even its most important. Crucially, an observer used a machine gun to defend his aircraft from enemy attacks. In October, Godfrey scored his first victory, from the observer's position in the front of a F.E.2b aircraft. Then he was accepted for pilot training in early 1917. He went through a training program in England similar to George Trim's, only at Netheravon for basic training and the University of Reading for

Capt. Earl Godfrey, centre in the front row, in command of the School of
Aerial Fighting at Beamsville, Ontario. Only Godfrey is identified by name
in this photo. Second from left in the back row is undoubtedly Lieutenant
George K. Trim. WILLIAM E. CHAJKOWSKY. ROYAL FLYING CORPS—BORDEN TO
TEXAS TO BEAMSVILLE. BOSTON MILLS PRESS. CHELTENHAM ON, 1979. P114

RFC Canada living under canvas at University College, University of Toronto. A Curtiss JN-4 (Can) flies over. CITY OF TORONTO ARCHIVES, FONDS 1244, ITEM 752

the School of Military Aeronautics.[13] He too would have found basic cadet training easy and, as a sergeant, would have been exempted from some of the service and duties required of raw recruits.

In the summer of 1917, Godfrey was flying a Nieuport scout in France with 40 Squadron and had thirteen victories. He was then transferred to England to fly a Sopwith Camel scout. With 44 Squadron, Godfrey's job was to fly night patrols to defend against Zeppelin airships and Gotha bombers that were attacking British cities. He was awarded the Military Cross in 1917, "For conspicuous gallantry and devotion to duty in constantly attacking hostile machines at close range, regardless of personal risk or of their being in superior numbers."[14] Godfrey ranks 323rd of 1,865 aces. Only 313 pilots— on both sides—shot down more aircraft in the whole of the war.

In March 1918, Godfrey was posted to Canada and the School of Aerial Gunnery in Beamsville. As we have seen, it was recognized by that period of the war that combat flying put great stress on pilots and they needed periods of rest, or at least duty away from combat. Although some pilots resisted posting away from the front, most recognized the need for a change.[15] In Beamsville, Godfrey's impact must have been immediate. He was daring flyer and a good shot. He was an ace—the real thing. He had also flown seventeen types of aircraft since joining the RFC. In July the SAG was renamed the School of Aerial Fighting, and in September 1918, he was appointed commander of the SAF.

The School of Aerial Fighting

Brigadier Cuthbert Hoare was the commander of the RAF in Canada. As described in Part Two, he was a charming and highly effective administrator who believed that he could expand training in Canada beyond basic flight. While the RFC was in Texas, Hoare had ordered the construction of the School of Aerial Gunnery, near

Beamsville, in the Niagara peninsula between Hamilton and Niagara Falls. Although he could not get the front-line fighters that such schools had in the UK, he pressed ahead. He did get one Sopwith Camel and made extensive use of the readily available Curtiss JN-4 (Can) aircraft being produced in numbers from the Canadian Aviation Ltd. factory in Toronto. The JN-4 could not be compared to a scout, but pushed to its limits, it could improve the skills of the cadets. With only one Camel available, and it being a single-seat machine, we might guess that it was not flown by cadets but reserved for instructors. Having to train in aerial tactics against a Camel in the hands of an ace would be quite an education.

Following the titles used in Britain, the Beamsville School of Aerial Gunnery was renamed the School of Aerial Fighting in July 1918. Cadets were living in tents during the summer as construction of the school went ahead. Alan Sullivan stated that by the Armistice, the SAF had built accommodation for 122 officers, 400 cadets, 96 warrant officers and sergeants, and 768 rank and file. In September, the SAF graduated 270 cadets each with more than 9 hours of flying time at SAF.

Frank Johnston—War Artist

Artists, as well as poets, were trying to convey the experience of flying. Paul Bewsher was one of the poets to do so, and one young Canadian artist attempted the same with painting. In 1918, Frank Johnston was a young artist from Toronto who had received a commission to paint the activities of the RAF Canada. In 1920, Johnston was a founding member of the Group of Seven. He received his commission from the Canadian War Memorials Fund, which was established in 1916 by Max Aitken (Lord Beaverbrook) to record Canada's war effort. Johnston visited most of the RFC/RAF aerodromes in Ontario and flew at several sites, including Beamsville.

ABOVE Training over Beamsville. Frank Johnston was among the first artists to try to depict the experience of flight. CANADIAN WAR MUSEUM 19710261-0243

OPPOSITE Frank Johnston was one of the earliest artists to depict the experience of flight. He wrote "Sopwith Camel Looping" on the back. There was one Camel at Beamsville, probably flown by experienced instructors, especially Godfrey. CANADIAN WAR MUSEUM 19710261-0254

THE SOPWITH CAMEL AT BEAMSVILLE DOING A LOOP.
THIS IS THE ONLY SOPWITH IN AMERICA AT THE PRESENT TIME.

He said of his experiences, "Flying... is very fine sport with the exception of the spinning nose dive."[16]

Johnston was fascinated with flight but faced an artistic challenge—how to portray the still new activity of flying. How could an artist capture the size of the sky, the smallness of the aircraft, and the beauty of the experience? His paintings, many based on photos he took, are technically accurate and painted on a large scale. In one, he included that Sopwith Camel fighter, so we know where that work was observed. The paintings were very popular and remain impressive over a century later.[17]

Godfrey was certainly an experienced Camel pilot, and we can easily speculate that as senior instructor he would have flown it regularly, and perhaps for the benefit of a visiting war artist. Trim's service record does not state that he qualified on the Camel though it does mention the Sopwith Pup. However, he may have flown the Camel as well—an instructor's privilege?

The Spinning Nose Dive—A Pilot's Worst Predicament

The aerial manoeuvre that so impressed Frank Johnston was, before 1916, a death sentence for pilots. Getting the plane out of the spin as it dived ever faster to the earth was a mystery. The Wright brothers had said before the war that ninety percent of all air fatalities resulted from a spinning nose dive. Only through trial and error was a solution found. According to Major Robert Smith-Barry of the RFC:

> Up to the autumn of 1916 not many pilots who had the misfortune to get into a spin in the air had ever regained control. One exception was Major J.A. Chamier who, while in France, found himself spinning as he came out of a cloud. While he was falling, he recalled an incident on Salisbury Plain before the war when Lt. W. Parke RN had recovered from a spin near the ground, when people crowded around to congratulate Lt. Parke on his luck, he

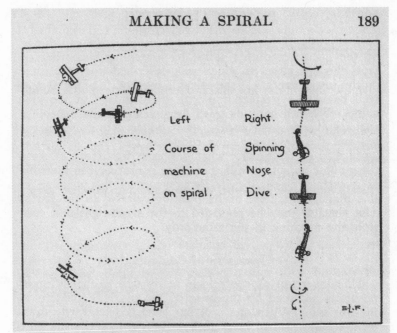

Left Right.

Course of Spinning

machine Nose

on spiral. Dive.

E.L.F.

The course followed by the machine in making a spiral descent, and what happens in a spinning nose dive.

Until the mystery was solved, the spinning nose dive was a death sentence.

AUTHOR'S COLLECTION. W.G. MCMINNIES. PRACTICAL FLYING. TEMPLE PRESS. LONDON, 1918

had explained that he had stopped spinning by doing "everything wrong." Maj. Chamier likewise did the opposite of what this experience as a pilot suggested and he also recovered. He subsequently related his adventure to Royal Flying Corps headquarters.[18]

The pilot in a spin was tempted to pull back on the control stick to pull up the aircraft. In fact, the opposite was the solution. Once pushing forward was discovered, the "stunt" was taught to all pilots in Britain, indeed it became a common manoeuvre in combat, as Billy Bishop described.

Billy Bishop eventually became the British Empire's leading ace, credited at the time with seventy-two victories in aerial combat. He described his first victory, in March 1917.

This was just at the time that the Germans were doing some of their famous falling stunts. They would go spinning down from great heights and just when you thought they were sure to crash they would suddenly come under control, flatten out into a correct flying position and streak for the rear of their lines. When my man fell ... into a spinning nose dive I dived after him. Down he went for a full thousand feet and then regained control."[19]

Bishop then shot him down.

The spinning nose dive became a standard part of a pilot's training, especially as part of the RFC's Gosport System. Developed by Major Robert Smith-Barry at Gosport Aerodrome in England, this system required well-trained instructors who would lead their pupils into more and more complicated manoeuvres, called stunts, simulating the flying required in combat. Student pilots in the Gosport System had fewer accidents and a better chance later of surviving in combat.[20] The training base at Gosport was named the School of Special Flying, and its graduates spread out to teach flying by the new methods. The spinning nose dive became a standard feature of training. Soon the Gosport System became the standard for training around the world.[21]

After Smith-Barry was injured in a crash, the School of Special Flying at Gosport was commanded by Duncan Bell-Irving of Vancouver.[22] His brother Richard was also in command of a training station—the School of Aerial Gunnery in Scotland. After the war, these two brothers played an important role in developing aviation in Canada. Duncan was a founder of the Aero Club of BC, a founder of the Air Cadets, and a founder of the RCAF auxiliary squadrons.

There were ten children in the Bell-Irving family of Vancouver—six brothers and a sister served in uniform, three in the RFC. Seated: Isabel and Richard, who commanded the School of Aerial Fighting in Turnberry, Scotland. Standing, left to right: Roderick (killed 1918), Henry, Aeneas, Malcolm, and Duncan. Duncan was an ace, with seven victories. VANCOUVER SUN, 8 NOVEMBER 2014. A DIVISION OF POSTMEDIA NETWORK, INC., AND ELIZABETH O'KIELY. GENTLEMAN ACE: THE DUNCAN BELL-IRVING STORY

In the Second World War he commanded several training schools for the RCAF.

In Canada, Brigadier-General Hoare established the School of Special Flying in North Toronto to train instructors in the Gosport System. When Trim and Godfrey arrived back in Canada in 1918, they would already have been trained in the Gosport System and they helped to advance the training methods of RAF Canada. The School of Aerial Fighting at Beamsville was modelled after the British schools commanded by the Bell-Irving brothers. As instructors at Beamsville, Trim and Godfrey would have been experts in the spinning nose dive.

War End—Major Earl Godfrey, MC, AFC

Shortly after the war ended, Godfrey was approached by Brigadier-General Hoare about flying over Niagara Falls. Hoare had not seen them, despite the fact that they were just down the road. Godfrey took the controls of the SAF's only Avro 504 trainer and took off, heading for the Falls at 1,000 metres. By banging on the fuselage and signalling by hand, Hoare seemed to indicate that he wanted to go lower. Godfrey obliged and dived right into the gorge and under the Honeymoon Bridge (where the Rainbow Bridge now stands). It was a move forbidden to cadets. On return to the SAF, Hoare was very angry, indeed frightened, but he soon forgave Godfrey, recommended him for the Air Force Cross, and wrote a very favourable report.[23]

Taking risks in the air, with or without the commanding general, was a part of life for the cadets and instructors. Visiting artists could be taken for a spinning nose dive. Cadets flew under bridges and buzzed cars. The RAF was not surprised—it had of course been looking for those with "the devil in them." Alan Sullivan even published photos of pilots standing and sitting on wings while in flight,

Alan Sullivan put the caption "Acrobatics" on this photo of a student pilot over Beamsville showing off on a Curtiss JN-4. Wing walking became one of the standard stunts of barnstorming pilots in the 1920s. ALAN SULLIVAN. AVIATION IN CANADA 1917–1918. P217

presenting the photos with captions such as "A centaur of the air," or "Pegasus."[24] There is a sense of pride in the lads. Within two years such practices would not be welcome in civilian flight.

At the end of the war, Godfrey briefly returned to England and was posted to 123 Squadron RAF, which became 2 Squadron CAF, one of the two squadrons of the short-lived Canadian Air Force. Although CAF was soon disbanded, Godfrey served, if only briefly, with some of the finest Canadian officers of the RAF. One of them was Donald MacLaren, who with Godfrey and a small group of men who knew each other from war service would dominate the early days of aviation in Canada. Godfrey had been hospitalized near the end of the war back in Canada and was again in May 1919 in Shoreham, England. He relinquished his commission on account of ill health in June and returned to Canada. Like many young men who had survived the war, he had to find a new life.

About the same time, George Trim was back in Vancouver, spinning and looping the loop for rapt audiences, racing a Curtiss JN-4 against Stutz cars and entertaining a Hollywood star.

Creating a World of Civilian Aviation

The Canadian government was unsure what to do about aviation after the war. It had disbanded the CAF, frightened by the cost, but many in Ottawa were aware that aviation could be an important new factor in both defence and civilian life. But few understood it, and some could see no use at all for aviation in peacetime.

Wary of the expense, yet also worried about control and safety, the government created an Air Board which would have a military arm—the recreated CAF—and a civilian arm. The goals were, "To control aeronautics, to attend to the licensing of pilots, the licensing and inspection of machines and the supervision of routes."[25]

A House of Commons committee called witnesses to hear suggestions about how to do this and to consider members for the Air Board. Several MPs thought that Billy Bishop, the greatest Allied ace and one of the most famous Canadians of the time, should be appointed to the board. General Mewburn, Minister of Militia, replied for the government. "At present Colonel Bishop was making something like $30,000 a month in the United States and there was not money enough in the Militia Department to induce him to act on the Board now, but he probably would be available later."[26] Bishop did not actually make that kind of money, but the sensationalism of the statement shows the attention that he received. He was not considered by the Air Board for any serious position.

The Air Board came into existence in June 1919, with Hugh Guthrie as chairman. Also on the board were the Deputy Postmaster

Donald MacLaren, 1919. He joined the RFC Canada in 1917 and after completing basic flying training in Ontario, was sent to England. As a Camel pilot, he shot down fifty-four enemy aircraft, tied for sixth among Allied aces, and ranked third among Canadian aces, behind Billy Bishop and Raymond Collishaw. He was the highest-scoring ace to come out of the Canadian training program. CITY OF VANCOUVER ARCHIVES. AM54-S4. P1674

ABOVE The Vancouver Branch of the Aerial League appealed for public support. ORIGINALLY APPEARED IN THE VANCOUVER SUN, 23 MARCH 1919. A DIVISION OF POSTMEDIA NETWORK, INC.

OPPOSITE Blythe Rogers. VANCOUVER PUBLIC LIBRARY. 2011-092.0030

General, the Minister of Naval Service, the Minister of Customs and Inland Revenue, and other worthies. Earl Godfrey was quickly employed by the board at its base at Jericho Beach in Vancouver[27] and was soon engaged in fisheries patrols in a flying boat. Later Godfrey would be in command of the base at Jericho Beach.

The Aerial League of Canada— "Aviation for Canada by Canadians"

While the federal government was trying to bring order and control to aviation, private citizens also took up the cause of advancing the business of flying. The Aerial League of Canada described itself as

> an association of far-seeing business men to foster aviation and the science of aerodynamics generally, to the end that Canada may occupy that proud place that she held gallantly in four years of war, and to keep evergreen the glorious memory of our flying men who fell after many a lone flight thousands of feet in the air, outnumbered, but game to the last.[28]

Two of the goals of the league were to demonstrate how aircraft could be applied to business and to find employment for Canadian aviators. Branches were established across Canada, each under appropriate provincial legislation for benevolent societies. Lifetime memberships were available for one hundred dollars.

George Taylor was the founder and president of the Vancouver branch of the league. He worked hard to recruit prominent men to become members. Two examples show the scope of Taylor's efforts. The honorary president was Sir Charles Hibbert Tupper, a former politician and federal cabinet member who had retired from politics to practise law in Vancouver. The formation of the league branch in Vancouver was endorsed in March 1919 by Premier John

Oliver, who contributed a hundred dollars and became a founder and patron of the BC branch.

Another of the prominent men to join the Aerial League was Blythe D. Rogers, president of the Rogers Sugar Refining Company. The company's name is still familiar to Canadians through Rogers Golden Syrup, then and now a widely used sugar product. Blythe Rogers was born in Vancouver in 1893 and was educated at exclusive private schools before entering the Royal Military College in Kingston, Ontario. When the war started, he was with the Second Division's Engineers. Before he could serve overseas, Rogers suffered a severe head injury in a riding accident in Ottawa and was discharged from the army.[29] He returned to Vancouver and the family business. Upon the death of his father, the company founder, Blythe assumed the position of president in 1918. This young, wealthy, and well-connected business leader would play an important part in George Trim's life in 1919 and 1920.

It was still the dawn of aviation and the league, with political, commercial, and social connections, was ready to bring enthusiasm into contact with Canadians.[30] Taylor had an ambitious program for the summer of 1919, including air shows, races, visits by league machines to the interior, and attempts at records.

While Godfrey had obtained a government job in aviation, there were not enough such positions to satisfy the desire to keep flying that energized many of the young men who had so recently learned to fly. There were no airlines. There were no airports—flyers had to use farmers' fields, beaches, parks. The aircraft available were military designs, and in any case, there were few large enough to carry passengers, never mind in comfort. What was a flying enthusiast to do?

His service record shows that Lieutenant Trim stayed with SAF Headquarters in Beamsville until at least January 1919. He formally left the service on 10 April and soon turned up in Vancouver, making a living as a flyer with the Aerial League of Canada.

The Vancouver branch of the Aerial League had announced in early May that they had arranged to buy four war surplus Curtiss JN-4 aircraft for the total sum of $7,200, plus cost of shipping from Toronto. The league already had one Curtiss machine. Blythe Rogers agreed to finance the purchase, and he was supported by other Vancouver business leaders.[31] The aircraft were shipped by rail from the Toronto aircraft factory, Ericson, which had taken over the wartime plant. There was also a special bonus for the league. They were given a fifth machine as part of the purchase, provided it be awarded to the winner of an air race. The winner, a league member of course, flying a league-owned machine, was expected to then give the prize to the league.[32] The Aerial League under George Taylor's leadership made sure that it, and its flyers, were constantly in the news.[33]

Barnstormers is the name given to itinerant flyers who travelled around North America, offering their services as entertainers. Organizers of fairs and exhibitions could hire the services of a flyer, enticing customers to pay admission to the fair to see the air show, meet the daring, perhaps even "dashing," airmen and inspect the machines that they flew. Most people outside cities had never seen an airplane. The barnstormers put on aerial shows, diving and looping above amazed crowds. They took paying customers for flights, and often carried cargo from place to place. The most common plane used by barnstormers in both Canada and the US was the Curtiss JN-4. They were available in the hundreds as war surplus. Flying the "Jenny," the barnstormers were soon showing off not just their flying skills but the stunts that they had performed while in the service, and this included wing walking. This was quickly recognized as reckless, even if popular. Were the young flyers addicted to danger as well as to flying?

Lieutenant George Trim—Showman

Press accounts show that the Aerial League's first show was on 10 May. Trim was described as an assistant pilot, and other league pilots were Captain Ernest Hoy, Captain Alfred Eckley (described as official test pilot), and a Lieutenant Foy. With that began George Trim's career as a civilian flyer, and a spectacular summer of stunts—and firsts.[34]

One of Trim's first assignments involved dropping a parachutist.[35] During the Great War, the balloon section was an important part of the RFC and RAF. Tethered balloons were used as observation posts, often at heights up to 1,500 metres. It was one of the jobs of fighter pilots to protect their own side's balloons from enemy attack, and of course to attack enemy balloons. When attacked, the balloonist would jump out with a parachute. RFC and RAF aircraft pilots did not have parachutes during the war, and Trim did not fly with one.

On 10 May, Comrades of the Great War, a veterans group, staged a homecoming celebration at the Cambie Street grounds in Vancouver. The Aerial League supplied Trim and a JN-4 to drop R.A. Carhart, "the famous balloonist," from approximately six hundred metres (2,000 feet) to land at the homecoming. He did so successfully, but in letting go, damaged Trim's plane; Trim had to cancel a planned one-man air show for the returned men and their families. The famous balloonist later that evening broke an arm and three ribs when he jumped from thirty metres (100 feet) and missed the safety net below.

On 3 June, the Aerial League staged an air race at Minoru Park in Richmond, BC. The location provided a grandstand for seating, a large open area for air operations, and easy access to Vancouver. Normally used for both horse and auto racing, Minoru Park was the centre of Vancouver flying shows for years. Trim raced Captain A. Eckley around the oval, each starting at opposite sides so they could fly at the same altitude.[36] Air races were popular everywhere that year. In August, a round-trip, two-day race from Toronto to New York City involved fifty aircraft and included Lieutenant-Colonel G.C. Barker, VC, one of Canada's greatest aces. One of the participants disappeared over Lake Ontario. In October, a race from New York to San Francisco saw seven fatalities. Flying races were popular, exciting, and dangerous.

The stunting was almost non-stop. On 22 June, the Aerial League arranged to have Trim start a lacrosse game at Queen's Park near Vancouver. Trim arrived over the park by "looping the loop followed by a spinning nose dive, and some hair-raising rolls," according to the *Daily World*. He then dropped a lacrosse ball from the air to start the game.[37] Clearly these stunts were widely popular and entertaining, and the spinning nose dive was among the common stunts.

The First Postwar Canada Day

It was called Dominion Day then, the celebration of Confederation, the creation of Canada and of what Canadians had accomplished, and 1 July 1919 was, of course, the first occasion for a national day of fun and games since the end of the war. Special events were organized coast to coast, and the day was also to be a grand chance to sell war bonds, to pay for the war. What better way to celebrate and to encourage people to buy bonds than an airshow, an aerial extravaganza? The Aerial League organized the show, and George Trim was one of the pilots at its centre.

Movie Stars and Flying

The films were silent and black-and-white, but the stars of Hollywood were as famous in 1919 as they are today. Thousands would

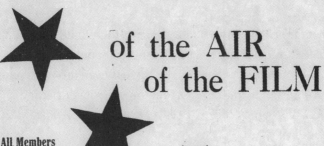

of the AIR
of the FILM

PRISCILLA DEAN

Universal Film Co.'s Super Star   *Coming from Los Angeles*

Her latest feature film showing week July 7th, Orpheum.

FLYING

Looping   *Spinning*   *Falling Leaf*   *Machine Brought down in Flames*
Whipping Richtofen's Red Air Fighters

PLENTY OF CARS to Minoru, Lulu Island Depot, Granville St. Bridge. Notice—Jitney Drivers start from bridge; 10,000 to haul.

DOMINION DAY

Minoru Park   *Special Cars Running*   *Granville Street Bridge*

Admission $1.00. Children under 12, free; over 12, 25c.

AERIAL WEDDING

Giant explosion, daring death flirtation. Man transferred from plane to auto, outdoing

DOUGLAS FAIRBANKS

Race, Stutz vs. airplane. Lacrosse. Dancing day and night. One hundred super attractions.

Official reception, SUPPER DANCE (informal), Vancouver Hotel, to Priscilla Dean, Monday evening, June 30th. Double tickets $3; single $2; ladies $1.00.

RAIN or SHINE   **FULL PROGRAMME**

Movie Stars and flying—celebrating on July 1, 1919. ORIGINALLY PUBLISHED IN THE VANCOUVER DAILY WORLD, 30 JUNE 1919. A DIVISION OF POSTMEDIA NETWORK, INC.

turn out to see them in person. The stars toured the continent to promote their movies and were paid for their appearances. Combine a popular star with war heroes, and there is even more attraction. As the *Winnipeg Tribune* in reporting the Vancouver event explained, the Aerial League "chose Priscilla Dean above all other stars to be the featured guest."[38]

Priscilla Dean was among the most famous stars of the era. She was even rumoured to have been secretly engaged to American ace and Medal of Honor recipient Eddie Rickenbacker.[39] Why not pair her with George Trim? The photos of the event at Minoru Park, from the Vancouver Archives, show her with Trim and his airplane, which she christened "Priscilla" before they took off. In all of the pictures, Trim seems to be enjoying himself tremendously. There he is after four years of military service—an aviator, a show attraction, and escorting a Hollywood star. What a life.

Appearing with Priscilla Dean was only one of Trim's jobs that weekend. He was also in a race—his Jenny against a Stutz racing car. This was a typical barnstorming stunt. Trim won.

George Taylor, the president of the Aerial League—perhaps fittingly in light of the stunts that the league arranged across Vancouver and indeed across BC—was married to Miss Caroline Allison in a ceremony that took place between two aircraft. The Vancouver *Province* reported the event.

> It was the first of its kind ever held in Canada and many of the spectators stayed on the grounds to witness the pleasing ceremony. The twelve bridesmaids, well-known Vancouver girls and pupils of Mr. Lionel Tucker of this city, and their partners all in the neat uniform of the Royal Air Force, made a pretty sight as they lined up around the bride and groom.[40]

The bride and groom then flew over the crowd of twelve thousand at Minoru Park.

George Trim and Priscilla Dean in front of his Aerial League machine. VAN-COUVER PUBLIC LIBRARY 17363

Living the life. George Trim and Hollywood star Priscilla Dean ready to take off.

The huge crowd at Minoru Park, near Vancouver, watching the stars of the air and the screen. VANCOUVER PUBLIC LIBRARY 17371

George Trim sitting in the Stutz car with driver Harry Hooper. The airplane won.

Priscilla Dean takes a turn posing in the Stutz racing car with driver Harry Hooper. STUART THOMSON PHOTOGRAPHER, VANCOUVER PUBLIC LIBRARY 17388

Scenes from Vancouver's First
Aerial Wedding at Minoru Park

This photo from the Vancouver *Province*, 3 July 1919, identified the bride and groom, centre, with G.K. Trim to the groom's right. George Taylor and his bride were willing to make a spectacle of their wedding. ORIGINALLY PUB-LISHED IN THE VANCOUVER PROVINCE, 3 JULY 1919. A DIVISION OF POSTMEDIA NETWORK, INC.

The same newspaper account of the wedding also praised Trim for his daring part in the air show.

The stunt flying was carried out by three machines piloted by Lieuts. G.K. Trim, "Minty" MacDonald, and Jack Clemence. They stayed up for well over forty minutes going through most of the stunts known to war flyers. Clemence and MacDonald climbed high up for their stunts and kept high, looking like mere specks in the sky to the spectators on the ground. Trim flew at 2000 feet in a silver-painted machine and did his stunts in bits at a time. He looped and then climbed back to his former height—he "stalled-turned" and again climbed, and so with all his stunts. Everybody could follow every move of the machine.

The League had scored a great triumph, and Trim too.

Trim Crashes on Way to Seattle

Just days after the triumphs of Dominion Day, the Aerial League sent Trim and another pilot on a flight to Seattle to put on a show for the Fourth of July celebrations. Trim ran into thick fog crossing the Strait of Juan de Fuca, lost his way for two hours, and made a forced landing in Washington State, on a beach eighty kilometres west of Port Angeles, with only half a gallon of gas left. A hard landing broke a wing strut and punctured the fuel tank. The other plane, flown by Captain Jimmie Gray, successfully entertained the American crowd for two hours.

There are two accounts in the press about how Trim got back to Canada. In the *Province*, he said he was fortunate to land near a First Nations community, and the people helped him repair the strut with a piece of driftwood and supplied him with gasoline so he could fly back across the strait to Victoria. However, the *Victoria Daily Colonist*, while enthusing about his successful return, left out the help he got.

> Lieut. Trim's brilliant work in landing on a beach, effecting repairs, cranking his bus and hopping off unassisted is only illustrative of the ingenuity which characterized the entire Royal Air Force during its grand war record.

The press could only have learned the details on this adventure from Trim himself. It was an exciting enough story and did not need myth building by the *Colonist*, but the RAF and flying still had mystique.[41]

This event only polished the bright image of George Trim in the public's eye and made him more famous in British Columbia. George Taylor must have been relieved at Trim's survival and, perhaps, very happy with the publicity.

New evidence emerged showing that not everyone was happy with the aerial and publicity stunts. In July, the Aerial League announced that it had no intention of organizing a trans-Canada flight, nor did it intend to have a flight under the Capilano Bridge. Taylor had clearly been promoting new adventures that the board of the league could not back. He offered to resign. The board of directors of the league asked him to stay on until the expected return of Donald MacLaren, another of the famous aces of the war. A publicity committee was created to be an official organ for liaison with the press, especially to issue denials of stories similar to the one about flying under the Capilano Bridge. At the same meeting, Blythe Rogers was thanked for his donation of five hundred dollars to be split between the league and soldiers' graves.[42] However, Taylor was not entirely "grounded."

In July, when Blythe Rogers and his wife flew over Vancouver, the *Vancouver Sun* reported,

> Although several benefactors of the Aerial League of Canada have taken flights over Vancouver, it is said that Saturday's passenger with Lieut. Minty Macdonald during the Peace celebration, Blythe D. Rogers, president of the B.C. Sugar Refinery, is the greatest.
>
> The five airplanes that were brought to this city were the direct result of Mr. Roger's support ... thus bringing a number of machines to British Columbia at an earlier date than would otherwise have been possible. Both Mr. and Mrs. Rogers were given "stunts" at the conclusion of the ride among the clouds.[43]

First Flight Across the Rockies

In August, the *Vancouver World* newspaper suggested that a flight be attempted between Vancouver and Calgary to "prove the commercial possibilities of the airplane. The matter was taken up with the Aerial League and Lieut. G.K. Trim was sent through to Calgary to report on the route of the proposed flight... Lieut. Trim reported favourably and Capt. E.C. Hoy, D.F.C., one of the most active members of the Aerial League, was selected to pilot the plane."[44] It was rumoured that the pilots drew lots for the job.

Captain Hoy had served in the RFC and RAF, becoming an ace with eight victories. He had been a part of the 1 July air show at Minoru Park, where he put on an aerial bombing demonstration. Hoy took off from Minoru Park on 7 August in one of the league's Curtiss planes and arrived in Calgary the same day, after intermediate stops for fuel. Thus, Hoy became the first to fly over the Rockies, and he was treated as a hero in Calgary. In a speech given at the civic reception, he predicted that the flights would become regular once more powerful machines were available. George Trim would play a central role in trying to do just that.

Today, reading between the lines, this appears to have been a publicity stunt arranged by the *Daily World*, the *Calgary Herald*, and the Aerial League. Nonetheless, it received great attention and helped focus public attention on aviation, and its potential.

On his return trip from Calgary, Hoy crashed in the town of Golden. He and his wrecked plane returned to Vancouver by train and, despite the setback, received a hero's welcome again. He blamed his crash on an inadequate landing field. Clearly there was much more to do to make commercial aviation viable.

This latest crash did not deter big plans which were announced on 13 August—an attempt at a cross-country flight. The *Victoria Daily Colonist* described the project.

Aerial League pilots posing with Capt. Hoy before the attempt to cross the Rockies. It was reported that they drew lots for the job. Capt. Hoy is sixth from left. "Minty" MacDonald is second from right. Second from left looks like George Trim. STUART THOMSON PHOTOGRAPHER, VANCOUVER PUBLIC LIBRARY 17367

First to cross the Rockies, British Columbia airmen are looking for further honors, and are planning a trans-Canada flight next month from Halifax to Vancouver. Lieut. Trim and Lieut. W.H. Welsh, two Vancouver men whose names are already well-known in flying, are preparing for a flight across the Dominion. They hope to make the distance in not more than forty hours. An attempt will be made to do the trip in thirty-six hours of actual flying time...

The machine to be used will probably be a de Havilland "4." According to the course mapped out, six stops will be made to advertise British Columbia spruce en route. To ensure the success of all arrangements connected with the flight, a company composed of men who have all seen service overseas has been formed, called The BC Trans-Canada Flight Association, with Mr. A.G. Imlay, secretary of the Aerial League of Canada, as President.[45]

Trim and Welsh said that organizers would include the Canadian Press, the Vancouver Board of Trade, and the Lumberman's Association.

It never happened. It's true that, just a month earlier, the league had reined in Taylor and said there were no such plans. Maybe Taylor had a hand in this and put Trim and Welsh up to the announcement, making a run around the board of directors. Some work behind the scenes had clearly been done to get sponsors, and the endorsement of the league's national secretary. That does seem to be beyond the experience of pilot George Trim. However, as the crashes by Hoy and Trim showed, there was more to overcome than just having a more powerful machine and some business sponsors. The infrastructure was primitive or just not there. Reality had to be faced.

Fighting Mosquitoes, Mapping Watersheds

What practical roles could airplanes play in the postwar world? Was there more to civilian flying than stunting? Many still thought them a gimmick or suited only for war.

Earl Godfrey was one of those trying to show a serious side to flying with his coastal patrols for the fisheries. Donald MacLaren worked with the Air Board to develop regulations for safe flying. Trim too did work that showed a practical use for aviation: he flew a federal government entomologist several times to survey mosquito breeding grounds. Mr. Hearle, the mosquito expert, said of his flight with Trim over the Fraser River valley, "In ten minutes aloft I made more progress with my map than I had in weeks on the ground." Trim made another flight with Mr. Hearle between Chilliwack and Mission, BC, after which Mr. Hearle was able to recommend draining part of a lake to eliminate what he considered the greatest mosquito breeding ground in the Lower Mainland. Hearle said that he looked forward to a time when aerial photography using large army cameras would produce complete and accurate maps.[46]

Trim accomplished another first when he piloted Major J.C. MacDonald on the first commercial aerial reconnaissance of a watershed in Canada. MacDonald was the provincial superintendent of construction in the Okanagan Valley near Vernon, BC, and he used his own camera to make the survey. MacDonald estimated that the aerial work would save six weeks to two months of work. Perhaps as important, it was reported that the rates for hiring Trim and the Aerial League plane were "reasonable."[47] This type of work would help find a useful role for the airplane in the 1920s, but did Trim find it boring? We can wonder if Mr. Hearle or Mr. MacDonald was treated to a spinning nose dive.

Trim's main occupation with the Aerial League for the rest of the year was barnstorming in the interior of BC in September and becoming more famous.

Trim Barnstorms BC

Captain Hoy gained lasting fame with his flight across the Rockies. Could George Trim top that? He spent the rest of the summer flying around British Columbia. He was credited with the first commercial air freight flight in BC, between Vancouver and Victoria.[48] He even held a record of forty-two minutes for that flight time, if only for one summer.[49] In September, press reports put him in Penticton, Vernon, Nelson, Kamloops, and Grand Forks, BC. These were long, solo flights across dangerous country. He often carried "mail" in the form of messages from one town's mayor to the next town. This was not official Post Office mail, but the messages showed the promise of commercial flight. Trim was a combined showman, courier, and freight agent.

A description of one of Trim's shows gives us an idea of the impact his barnstorming for the Aerial League had that year. The language is flowery and over the top by our standards today, but worth the read to get a sense of what people thought of flying and of George Trim.

From the *Vancouver Daily World*, 22 August 1919:

AERIAL STUNTS THRILL KELOWNA
(WORLD SPECIAL SERVICE)

Thrilling the thousands who thronged the beach at Kelowna on Thursday by some hair-raising stunts in the air, Lieut. Trim captivated all who saw him. Vociferous cheers greeted him at the termination of the exhibition as an expression of the praise which he merited for the excellence of his performance.

The public had almost given him up when he put in an appearance for he had been expected on the Wednesday... but when he was sighted, flying well over 8000 feet high, coming across the mountains on the west side of the lake, the people forgot their previous disappointment and greeted the aviator with cheers of welcome. In response to these, when right over the water, he gave an exhibition of rolls, spins, and nose dives, before making for the landing ground two miles or more away for the replenishment of his gas supplies.

Then he came back again, and truth to tell everybody thought it was going to be a mediocre exhibition. For all he did for a few minutes was to circle around in front of the grandstand and over the city. But soon he began to mount higher and higher and yet higher and then the thrills began. He was no laggard when it came to doing breath-taking stunts and the spectators had enough thrills to furnish them with conversation for months to come. In one nose dive he made five complete turns before coming to a level position again and the graceful manner in which he did this showed he was complete master of his machine and without the slightest fear. Rolls, flying upside down, and the many exhibitions which many had read about, but few had seen were brought off without hesitation and then he put up a few jokes on those who had secured points of vantage from which to view the flight. The chief of these was the diving stand in the water and coming at lightning speed he passed at only about twelve feet over this, and the small boys who had climbed up there instinctively ducked, to the amusement of all who were in the grandstand and on the beach. Then he passed his attention on to those in motor and row boats and passing only some twelve of fifteen feet over the water's surface he caused the people in the craft also to duck. All in all, it was a magnificent exhibition and when it was about over the cheers broke out afresh and Lieut. Trim was the hero of the hour. On Friday Lieut. Trim carried passengers on short trips.

And so it went on, from town to town. On 9 September 1919: "Lieut. Trim of the Vancouver Aerial League has endeared himself to the hearts of all Okanagan people by the excellence of his flying exhibitions and the care with which he takes his passengers into the Empyrean." In Grand Forks, the mayor declared a civic holiday so people could attend Trim's show. Trim said he had to use both hands in greeting people, there were so many hands to shake.

Meeting Royalty

One of the biggest national events of 1919 was the cross-country tour of Edward, the Prince of Wales. Patriotic feelings in English-speaking Canada were still firmly entwined with Britain and the royal family. The prince was very popular, and his visits attracted large happy throngs. Only in later years would he become a contro-versial character after abdicating the throne to marry the woman he loved. Towns were decorated with patriotic flags, and parades and banquets were held wherever he went. The *Kelowna Record* reported, "Lieut. Trim flew in his aeroplane over the royal train as it arrived at Kamloops and was afterwards presented to His Royal Highness."

The Kamloops paper said, "Lieut. Trim, during his three-day engagement here was easily the great attraction of the fair... and his nose dives, spirals, Immelmann turns, and loops were thrilling in the extreme to the spectators. His reputation obtained in the Puget Sound Derby, and in the time flights between Vancouver and Vic-toria was fully maintained, in the opinion of critics in Kamloops."

The highlights of the fall fair were the Prince of Wales and George Trim in his Curtiss JN-4. Clearly, flying caught the imagina-tion of the population. Wherever he went, George Trim was treated like a hero. He must have felt he was on top of the world.

A Watery Crash

After three days of show in Nelson, on 25 September, Trim crashed again, this time directly into Kootenay Lake. The press report stated:

Although Nelsonites and fair visitors waited patiently for a considerable time yesterday to catch a glimpse of the stunting aviator, Lieut. G.K. Trim, and his plane, they were doomed to disappointment. Upon taking off for his flight the machine ran into a calm spot in the atmosphere with the result that there was not sufficient length of runway to allow him to rise and he landed 75 feet out in the lake.

As the undercarriage and lower part of the fuselage struck the water the machine upended and turned over and then fell back sticking in the mud at an angle of 75 degrees. The aviator, though badly shaken up for the time, was not submerged and loosened himself from his seat. Ropes were then secured by the crowd which had collected to see the airman rise and the machine, after considerable difficulties had been overcome, was pulled ashore.[50]

To Trim and the other Aerial League pilots, the crashes were a normal part of the job. Perhaps crashing was as normal for them as doing a spinning nose dive.

The End of the Flying Season, 1919

With the approach of winter, the flying season came to an end. Although the RAF Canada had pioneered winter flying in 1917-18, it was not yet practical in the civilian world. The Vancouver Aerial League had finished a successful season publicizing aviation and creating a form of air mindedness. It ended the flying season with a general meeting in October. George Taylor retired as president and was made an honorary life member and honorary vice-president. He was eased out the door, with recognition for his services. The new president was General Victor Odlum.[51] This was a brilliant move for the League. Odlum was wealthy and connected. He was a war hero, having risen to the rank of brigadier-general. His later career as a politician, soldier, and diplomat proved his abilities and

Trim with his Curtiss shortly after crashing into Kootenay Lake. He was unhurt, but the plane did not fly again that year. The plane is still painted with RAF markings, possibly 90 Canadian Training Squadron. THE KUTNE READER

influence. His involvement in Vancouver journalism as a newspaper publisher and owner helps to explain the attention that aviation and the league would keep getting in the coming year. Also elected was Captain Hoy, hero of the Rockies flight, and Blythe Rogers, whose presence ensured continued financial connections.

There were other changes in the wind as well. The barnstorming, aerial races, and constant stunts were not what many leaders, among them members of the Aerial League, wanted for the future of aviation. In addition, the Air Board, with a whole other view of aviation, was beginning to exert control.[52]

George Trim had a foot in both camps. He was now both a showman and a promoter of the development of civilian commercial aviation. He had carried mail and freight and flown for surveys and mapping, but he had also raced and put on air shows. Perhaps above all, Trim loved flying. He worked within a small community of veteran flyers, all of them dedicated like him to flying and promoting the future of aviation. They had contacts and close aviation friends across the country. They were the very foundation of Canadian civilian aviation.

George Trim—Entrepreneur

The 1920 flying season had great promise. One of the first changes was that the Aerial League went out of the actual business of flying planes. On January 3, the *Vancouver Daily World* announced that Lieutenant Trim had purchased four Curtiss planes from the Aerial League: "Lieut. Trim states that he intends to establish a flying school at Minoru Park and to engage in general commercial aviation." The *Vancouver Sun* noted that the planes were all Curtiss JN-4s and two of them had been recently overhauled. The others had

> suffered more or less severe crashes since they were brought
> to Vancouver. The planes... have played a big part in making

flying history in British Columbia. Numbered among them is the first plane to cross the Rockies, the first plane to penetrate the interior of the province and the first plane to brave the pass of the Coquahalla [sic].[53]

It is almost certain that Trim himself did not buy these machines, as events later in the year show. In the announcement of Trim's "purchase" of the airplanes, the *Vancouver Sun* also summarized his career in 1919.

> Lieut. Trim has to his credit the first trip into the interior of the province and a number of flights in the course of which he gave the inhabitants of the upper country their first sight of an aeroplane.

Trim was in the thick of things aerial as 1920 started.

Early in the new year, the Vancouver Aerial League ran into some bad publicity at the hands of its founder and recently departed president, George Taylor. In February, police charged that Taylor had collected money, supposedly for the league, without consent of the league and had continued to do so after he had left office.[54] This news suggests that the new leadership of the league had not only sold its machines and gotten out of the flying business, but also cleaned house. The fraud case, and Taylor, soon disappeared from the press.

The Canadian Air Service Association

The Canadian Air Service Association (CASA) was formed in January 1920 by air force veterans organizations in the four western provinces. The president was Capt. Fred McCall, another ace, with many other famous flyers on the board of directors, including Capt. "Wop" May, who had been in the "dogfight" when the famous Baron von Richthofen was shot down. May was also an ace and had a famous career as a barnstormer and a bush pilot.

The purpose of CASA was to act as a veterans' association and to support all projects related to aviation. The CASA goals were "to cement and continue close friendships formed between ex-members of the RAF, to promote an interest in all aerial navigation, to undertake aerial races and competitions and to secure employment for members." All members had to be veterans of the RAF. The new organization was ready to take up the stunts that the Aerial League seemed to be leaving behind. There were a thousand members in BC, and three hundred in Vancouver. George Trim was elected as a director of the BC branch of CASA on 5 March 1920.[55]

CASA also made clear to the Air Board in Ottawa that all future appointments to provincial Air Boards in the west should go to CASA members. This may seem to be a rather bold demand for jobs, but CASA was met with a sympathetic, even co-operative ear. The Air Board's new regulations came into effect on 1 January 1920, imposing government controls on aviation. Major Donald MacLaren spoke to the founding CASA conference and outlined the new role of the Air Board. He proposed an official role for CASA as an advisor to the Air Board on all aeronautical activities. MacLaren imagined the Air Board as a partner, not just an enforcer of regulations.[56]

MacLaren Outlines the Future of Aviation

In February, MacLaren released a report to the Air Board of his vision for the future. The Vancouver *Province* took up the story on 2 February.

VANCOUVER ACE SUBMITS RECOMMENDATIONS
TO AIR BOARD. POINTS OUT VALUE OF
AERIAL SURVEY AND PROTECTION WORK IN B.C.

There is probably no state or province which lends itself so completely to the development by air of its natural resources as British

Columbia. The chief public services which can be rendered by aircraft in British Columbia are mail carriage, fishery patrolling, forest ranging, exploratory surveying, photo topographical surveying, customs inspection, mounted police, inland revenue patrolling, and coast guard work.

MacLaren believed that flying boats and seaplanes would be the required aircraft, given the geography of the province. MacLaren continued to see a partnership between the Air Board and private enterprise. He pointed out that with the industry so new and undeveloped, it could not develop on its own.

"It is also hoped that support will be given by the citizens of this province to the companies which undertake to carry out air services by carrying mails, passengers and goods"[57]

MacLaren's report was widely covered in the newspapers and showed the hopes that so many were still putting into this new technology.

The Pacific Aviation Company

On 30 March, at the age of twenty-five, George Trim became the managing director of the Pacific Aviation Company, the first commercial aviation company in British Columbia.[58]

The company was legally incorporated on 1 April 1920 with a capitalization of one hundred thousand dollars. Company president was Blythe Rogers, the vice president was R. Marpole, and the secretary-treasurer was J.L. Gregg, president of CASA. The company was formed "for the purpose of the promoting of commercial aviation throughout the province." The *Daily World* said it was the only concern operating land machines in the province.[59]

Clearly, Blythe Rogers, who had funded the Aerial League's acquisition of machines in 1919, was a power behind the scenes. He provided the access to capital and experience in business operations which the flyers lacked. But Rogers never saw the results of the chance he took on flying and on Trim. He suddenly died, age twenty-seven, on 6 May. The death of this influential young business leader was a shock in Vancouver. His obituary suggested that his death was the result of his war injury, and the effects of influenza and pneumonia the previous winter. His brother Ernest stepped into his shoes at BC Sugar, and the Pacific Aviation Company also continued.

Aviation companies were springing up all over Canada. Most were small operations, with only one or two aircraft, usually war surplus Curtiss JN-4 Canucks. The Air Board's registration system preserved the history of some of these machines. For example, RAF Curtiss machine C574 became machine G-CACJ of the Commercial Aviation School in Victoria. RAF Curtiss machine C206 became machine G-CAAG, registered to Pacific Aviation Company on 27 April.[60]

The most famous of the new companies was probably Bishop-Barker Aeroplanes Limited, which was incorporated in Ontario in November 1919, with three hundred thousand dollars capitalization. Billy Bishop and Bill Barker, both Victoria Cross holders, were definitely the most famous aviators in Canada. They too attracted well-known investors, and their first machine was also a war surplus Curtiss JN-4, registered as G-CAAT.[61]

In another press conference, Trim announced that the company would operate four Curtiss JN-4s and two Avro machines, which were on order. Trim said that the Avros would be "bigger and more powerful than any yet seen around Vancouver" and be capable of carrying a pilot and two passengers. The company would operate out of Minoru Park, and Trim said he planned to "engage actively in the flying game." He also announced that he had hired several local airmen as pilots, including Major A.C. Baker AFC. Routes and schedules were being planned for flights to Victoria, Seattle, and "points throughout the interior."[62]

The company certainly got press attention, and with George Trim as managing director, it would remain in the limelight. In the middle of April, the *Vancouver Sun* announced that CASA and the Pacific Aviation Company would hold a joint meet at Minoru Park on 24 May "for the purpose of furthering the interest in aviation and as a demonstration of the possibilities of air service from a commercial point of view."[63]

The enthusiasm for aviation was not without words of caution. At a dinner arranged for RAF veterans, Colonel Richard Bell-Irving, who had commanded the School of Aerial Gunnery in Turnberry, Scotland, was the guest speaker. For his wartime services, Bell-Irving had been made a Commander in the Order of the British Empire. This was an award created in 1917 to recognize the contributions to the war of people in support roles, such as air training. It was his brother who had helped develop the Gosport system of pilot training.

Bell-Irving addressed Major MacLaren's report about the future of aviation. He pointed out that without air parks, depots, and communications between these and aircraft, caution should be exercised. He recommended that private enterprise "not get in too deep" until government had supplied the basic infrastructure. Bell-Irving also warned companies that planned to carry passengers that they should ensure their pilots were qualified flyers who would comply with regulations regarding the safety of passengers. He also urged the amalgamation of the Aerial League and CASA. Despite this caution, the report of this dinner carried in the *Vancouver Daily World* on 10 April could not disguise the enthusiasm of the gathered veterans for flying.

At the end of April, the Air Board granted Pacific Aviation the first commercial aviation licence issued in BC. The superintendent of certificates, Colonel J.S. Scott, required that the company complete a return flight to Chilliwack and a night flight in and out of Minoru Park. For both, Trim was the pilot and flew a Curtiss JN-4. Again, the press took notice, and on 28 April, the *Daily World* was almost poetic.

The hum of a motor in the sky, followed by the flash of an aeroplane's wings as the machine passed through the rays of the moon, caused many pedestrians to stop and look into the heavens last night about 8:30 o'clock. The machine presented a pretty picture as it sailed through the air.

It was the first night flight over Vancouver, and Lieut. G.K. Trim of the Pacific Aviation Company was the pilot.

A demonstration of day and night-flying, taking-off and landing followed by an inspection of the machines and hangars and the Pacific Aviation Company was granted the first commercial aviation licence to be issued in British Columbia.[64]

Colonel Scott was also testing pilots, and Trim was the first of twelve Vancouver pilots tested to pass and be issued a commercial pilot's licence. Only Trim was mentioned in the papers. A condition of having a pilot's licence was that the pilot be available to serve in the Canadian air force.

Train Chasing

Trim had no need for a PR consultant—he seemed to be a natural. A day after he was licensed, the papers reported Trim's next triumph. Actor Patrick Ludlow had missed his train to Calgary where he was scheduled to perform. Ludlow hired Pacific Aviation and Trim to fly him ahead of the train, to catch it at its next stop. The *Daily World* reported Trim's account.

We knew the train would reach Kamloops at seven o'clock and there was plenty of time... I took off and headed into the Coquahalla [*sic*] Pass. Meantime the wind had turned against us and when we neared the pass it grew dark and stormy and we could

Pacific Aviation advertised to attract attention and customers. ORIGINALLY
PUBLISHED IN THE VANCOUVER SUN, 15 MAY 1920. A DIVISION OF POSTMEDIA NET-
WORK, INC.

make little headway. Accordingly, I was forced to turn around and
make for home.

The *Daily World* added, "The pilot deplored the fact that Vancouver had taken so little interest in aviation as to make the Curtiss the
only type of machine available in such a crisis." Trim said, "With
a modern high-powered bus we would not need to go through the
storm in the pass. We could have ridden over it." Newspapers across
the country picked up the dramatic story.[65]

Day after day, in late April and through May, Trim and Pacific Aviation were in the newspapers. He had other pilots working for him and they too got publicity. Major Baker dropped from the air five hundred free tickets to the opening game of the baseball season.[66] The press announced that Trim was replacing his order for Avro machines with one for a Bristol "Tourer" because the Avros were not going to arrive that season. The Tourer was being sent from New York. Another of Trim's public relations flights involved two singers from the Sonora Grand Opera on a half-hour flight over Vancouver—covered of course by the papers.[67] Then, one evening just four days before the heavily advertised meet at Minoru Park, both Trim and Baker "spiralled and stunted" over Vancouver for forty-five minutes and got more newspaper coverage.[68]

With constant press coverage of Pacific Aviation, the investors must have been delighted with Trim. The financial records of the company may eventually be found to tell us if there was any real business income from all of this, but Blythe Rogers and the other backers invested must surely have been looking to the long run, and the future of flying.

The Big Meet—May 24, 1920

At Minoru Park, Lieutenant Trim and Major Baker were taking passengers up for a ride over the city of Vancouver. The manager of the Union Steamship Company, E.H. Beazley, had lunched at the Shaughnessy Club with his wife and friends, then driven to Minoru Park to watch the flying and the polo.[69] Beazley was reportedly unsure about going up for a trip, but his wife had just returned from a flight with Major Baker. Mr. Beazley was persuaded—he suited up, and climbed into Baker's Curtiss machine.

The *Vancouver Sun* described what happened next.

Pacific Aviation's crashed Curtiss JN-4, 24 May 1920. Vancouver photographer Stuart Thomson took this photo at Minoru Park showing the front seat where Beazley was killed. STUART THOMSON. CITY OF VANCOUVER ARCHIVES, AM1535-: CVA 99-3310

Another view of the crashed machine, taken by Stuart Thomson. E.H. Beazley was Vancouver's first air fatality. His wife, who had just completed a flight, was an eyewitness. STUART THOMSON. CITY OF VANCOUVER ARCHIVES, CVA 99-3309

During the war, Curtiss machines were often in crashes. The cadet pilot in the front seat was in the most dangerous position, often dying while the instructor behind survived. This machine crashed in Ontario in the winter of 1917–18. The photographer, James Crookall of Vancouver, was a corporal in an IRFC crash team. JAMES CROOKALL, CROOKALL FONDS, CITY OF VANCOUVER ARCHIVES. ITEM AM640-S1-: CVA 260-1130.02

The plane presented a beautiful spectacle with the light reflecting from its silvered wings and with the blue sky for a background. Suddenly the machine went into a nose spin when almost above the flying field, and spectators who knew Major Baker as a flyer remarked on it being unusual for him to attempt anything in the way of stunts in a plane of the kind he was piloting. The machine continued its spiral descent each circle growing larger and when onlookers had counted 15 or 16 of these circles, anxiety rose as to its control.[70]

The plane hit the ground within sight of the grandstand at Minoru Park, and of Mrs. Beazley. Mr. Beazley was in the front seat (usual for passengers) and was killed, dying at the scene. Baker survived but was badly concussed and cut on the face. He was rushed to hospital. This was the first air fatality in Vancouver.

Coroner's Inquisition

A coroner's inquest, then called an inquisition, was held the next day. Baker was still in hospital and not fit to attend. George Trim was called as a witness. Events were still very fresh in his mind, less than a day after the event.

Coroner: Tell the jury what you know of this case.

Trim: I saw Mr. Beazley getting into Major Baker's machine. They took off and went over town and they were approximately 20 or 25 minutes away and they returned at an altitude I should say of between 4,000 and 4,500 feet. The machine and engine went all right and suddenly it turned into a vertical bank and was put into a nose dive, a spinning nose dive, for four or five turns. The machine spun perfectly and then it didn't seem to come out. They tried to get it out in a kind of a bigger circle, a slower circle, and after a couple of times I realized there was something wrong and I immediately went in Mr. Hindes car and jumped in and we were on the way to the scene of the accident before the machine touched the ground. On my arrival there was a lot of people there getting Mr. Beazley out, Major Baker first and they rushed him to the hospital and got Mr. Beazley out and someone asked whether he was alive or dead and they said he was dead. I examined the controls of the machine and found the controls in perfect order. There was not a control wire broken. The only wires that were broken were those that fastened the centre section to the fuselage of the machine and that, as you will see by the photographs of the crash, when the plane hit the ground, the plane went forward and naturally something had to give way and that was the only wire broken as far as I know. The Chief of Police was there and examined the controls with me.

Coroner: What experience has Major Baker had in the operation of machines?

Trim: In this special type of machine?

Coroner: Yes.

Trim: He has flown four or five hours with this particular machine, but something like 2700 hours during his career.

Coroner: This particular type of machine was new to him wasn't it?

Trim: Well, it was something new, but a man that has flown in several different kinds of machines finds very little difference.

Coroner: How long have you known Major Baker?

Trim: About two months.

Coroner : Only in B.C. here?

Trim: Only in B.C.

Coroner: Is he under you, or who is the head?

Trim: I am the managing director of the Pacific Aviation Company.

Coroner: And he is under your directions?

Trim: Yes.

Coroner: Is there any examination necessary before you allow him to carry passengers or drive a machine at all?

Trim: Yes, I tested Major Baker myself and let him go up alone, and he flew for an hour alone before he ever took passengers, a couple of hours in fact, that day.

Coroner: And you consider him a fairly competent man?

Trim: I consider Major Baker a very good pilot.

Coroner: Major Baker was an instructor, was he?

Trim: He was O.C. in the flying school, officer commanding.

Coroner: From the way it came down, could you form any idea of whether it got into an air pocket or not, or why it should fall?

Trim: No, I don't think so. The machine spun perfectly as I say for about the first five turns. I go up every day and spin down in the machines perfectly safely.

Coroner: It looked as though when it came to the nose dive it was put that way?

Trim: Yes, I think so. I think it was put into a nose dive.

Coroner: You have the idea that if he had not been putting it into a nose dive that it might have landed in the ordinary way?

Trim: Yes, I think so.

George Trim was the main witness, with the lengthiest testimony. Mechanics from Pacific Aviation testified that the controls of the machine were in good order before and after the crash, and another witness described Major Baker as a careful pilot not given to stunting.[71] It appears that a spinning nose dive was not considered stunting by Trim or Baker.

The coroner suggested that the jury wait until Baker could testify, but the jury insisted on immediately returning a verdict of death by accident.

Who Was Major Baker?

Major Baker is something of a mystery man. The *Vancouver Sun* reported his name as Albert C. Baker, but there was no such person in the RAF. There is an Alfred Clifford Baker in RAF records, but he was killed in 1918. It was not unusual for newspapers to spell names incorrectly, but the only Baker to fit the bill in the RAF is not a viable candidate.[72]

Major Earl Godfrey Baker, AFC—that indicates he had been awarded the Air Force Cross, a prestigious medal for non-combat service—had been awarded the AFC for his leadership at the School of Aerial Fighting. But there is no A.C. Baker listed among those awarded the AFC.

There are just a few tantalizing hints in other public records. A.C. Baker appears later in the 1920s as an aeronautical engineer in Seattle, and American draft records for A.C. Baker state he has a scar on his lip, which we might guess came from a crash.

The publication *American Aeronautics—Aviation* (volume 12, 1922), gives a biography of a Major Albert Clifford Baker, born in England in 1897, educated at the Maidstone Technical and Engineering College, and joining the army in 1914 at the age of seventeen. This bio says Baker transferred to the RFC in 1915, shot down twenty-two aircraft, and was awarded the Military Cross in

December 1914, the DFC in 1917, and the AFC in 1917. He was discharged as a major. His address is given as Vancouver.[73]

This would appear to be our man, but experts in RAF service note that he is not listed among those with the Military Cross, and that the DFC and AFC did not exist in 1917. The Aerodrome website and *Above the Trenches*—both respected sources on aces—do not list an A.C. Baker as an ace. None of the Bakers listed as aces shot down as many aircraft, none have the right biography, and none were "A.C."[74] It has also been suggested that biographies in *American Aeronautics* were submitted by the person and not checked.

Another problem is Trim's claim in his testimony that Baker had flown 2,700 hours. This may be a typo in the transcript. It is a tremendous number. If Baker had flown six hours a day, it would have taken him 450 days to accumulate that number of hours. Surely Trim would have questioned that number.

So, there is no definitive record, and the lack of a Baker in the list of holders of the AFC especially raises the question of an "embellished" war record. But would Trim have been fooled? Would the dozens of veteran RAF pilots in Vancouver have been fooled? The second crash inquiry must have put Baker to the test.

The Air Board Investigation

The Air Regulations were brand new, having come into force on 1 January 1920. Pilots had to be licensed, and the qualifications for commercial pilots and testing were clearly set out. The section on dangerous flying was so short that it bears looking at in its entirety.

Part IX—Dangerous Flying

92. No aircraft shall fly over any city or town except at such an altitude as will enable the aircraft to alight outside the city or

town should the means of propulsion fail through breakdown or other cause.

93. No person in any aircraft shall

(a) carry out any trick flying over any city or town area or populous district; or

(b) carry out any trick flying or exhibition flying over any regatta, race meeting, or meeting for public games or sports, except when especially arranged for in writing by the promoters of such regatta or meeting; or

(c) carry out any flying which, by reason of low altitude or proximity to persons or dwellings, is dangerous to public safety; or

(d) drop or cause or permit to be dropped from an aircraft any article capable of causing injury or damage, or any ballast except water or fine sand.[75]

If the Air Board was to bring safety and order to civilian aviation, they would need to exercise their authority, and there was no better forum than to investigate fatalities. An inquiry was commissioned with Major Clarence "Claire" MacLaurin, the superintendent of flying operations for the Air Board in BC, as its chair. The other members were Stanley Taylor, the most experienced JN-4 pilot available, and Lieutenant-Colonel Richard Bell-Irving, who had issued words of caution in April.[76]

Claire MacLaurin was one of the first graduates of the Curtiss Flying School in Toronto in 1915 and joined the Royal Naval Air Service as a pilot of flying boats. He had also served in administrative posts in Washington and Ottawa and became interested in the development of postwar civil aviation. In 1919, he had written an important memorandum that influenced the role of the federal government in developing and regulating aviation.

DATE	PLACE	MARKINGS	TYPE	OWNER	PILOTS	PASSENGERS	REMARKS
3-5-20	Saskatoon, Sask.	G-CAAJ C	Curtiss	McClelland & Lobb	H.L.Lobb Injured	R.C.Hamilton Killed	Pilot put machine in spin and could not recover in time. His certificate was suspended for three months and cancelled owing to his being permanently unfit for flying.
5-5-20	Saskatoon, Sask.	Curtiss C.T		Keng Wah Aviation School	Lin On Injured	---	Accident due to lack of experience part of pilot.
24-5-20	Vancouver, B.C.	G-CAAF C	Curtiss	Pacific Aviation Co.	A.C.Baker Injured	E.H.Beasley Killed.	Accident due to lack of experience the part of the pilot with this particular type of machine.
							Forced landing due to engine fail...

Archivists at Library and Archives Canada searched for the Air Board Report. All that remains is this summary. Note that the two prior reports of accidents also involved Curtiss machines, one involved a spin, and all noted lack of pilot experience. LIBRARY AND ARCHIVES CANADA

> The United States is preparing a gigantic Aircraft policy. Practically every other country in the universe is awake to the possibilities and is preparing a progressive programme. Should Canada not have a National Service, a service embodying all the principal branches, a public utility in connection with aeronautics and an industry that will, within a few years, compare with motorcar building, ship building, or even railroading?

MacLaurin was a believer and true pioneer of Canadian aviation.[77]

This was an experienced, prestigious panel. If Baker was a fraud, surely he would be exposed. If there had been negligence, this panel of aviation experts would expose it. This was much more serious for the future of those involved and for aviation in Canada than a coroner's inquisition.

It has been assumed for decades that the first Air Board investigation was conducted in Vancouver in August of 1920.[78] This error was created because the report of inquiry into the Baker–Beazley crash no longer exists. The actual report, said in the press to have been sent to Ottawa, is not with Library and Archives Canada there. An exhaustive search in 2020 by archivists at LAC has turned up only a list of early accidents and of the reports filed, including this one. But the report itself has been lost. The sensational nature of the accident, however, ensured that the press covered the investigation, and from news accounts we can gather the following.

Major MacLaurin framed the purpose of the investigation as intending "to improve flying in Canada and to make it absolutely safe, and to safeguard against similar accidents in future."[79]

Much to the annoyance of the press, the investigation was held in camera, as the Air Board considered the technical matters to be too complicated for an open public meeting. There were, however, leaks. In one, on 31 May, the *Province* said that Baker had amnesia and could remember nothing of what happened. His doctor had "forbidden that anyone should broach the subject to him in his present state." The other leak, on 5 June in the *Province*, purported to be a statement from Baker in which he described what happened. Baker said he had seen Beazley make a spinning motion to dive with his hand, so he put the machine into a perfect dive, but was unable to straighten the rudder bar. He broke the heels off his shoes trying to move the bar. He even let go of the stick and tried to use his hands on the bar, but to no avail. But there is a problem with Baker's claim. Would a man who was making his first flight, who had been hesitant to fly in fact, have signalled for a spinning nose dive?

The Air Board announced its findings in early July, after hearing three days of secret testimony.

News reports quoted parts of the report:

In as much as it is the policy of the Air Board to foster and encourage commercial aviation at present in its infancy and conscious of the duty that the board owes to such enterprises . . . and to protect the public . . . the inquiry was conducted along the most searching lines.

The accident was caused by the pilot, Major A.C. Baker AFC, flying and putting aircraft G-CAAF into a spin in contravention of Air Regulations 1920 and owing to his inexperience in this type of machine, being unable to regain normal flight.[80]

As well, Baker did not have a commercial pilot's licence although Trim and the other pilots of Pacific Aviation did. Furthermore:

Pacific Aviation is to blame for its neglect to abide by or to enforce the air regulations throughout its operations.

George Trim was not named, but as managing director, the blame surely fell directly on him.

The Aftermath

Maj. D.B. Hobbs of the Air Board said, on 6 July, that it could strictly enforce regulations which included a maximum fine of a thousand dollars and/or six months in jail. But the Air Board said it saw no cause for such imposition.[81] Perhaps the coroner's verdict of accident complicated matters. No mention was made of Baker.

That was the end of Pacific Aviation. It disappeared. George Trim also left the public eye. There is a brief press report of him crashing in Agassiz on 2 July,[82] at the same time that the Air Board report was released, but after that, he and Pacific Aviation do not appear in the press. Nothing is heard again of Baker.

The second air fatality in Vancouver occurred later that summer on 18 August. Captain Hibbert Brenton, who had served in the RNAS and RAF, crashed a seaplane into English Bay. His two brothers had been killed in the war, and his sister witnessed his crash. Like Beazley, Brenton was also an employee of the Union Steamship Company.[83] Brenton had been in the same squadron as Claire MacLaurin, who inspected the crashed plane the next day. MacLaurin told reporters that Brenton had been a careful, cautious pilot, and he suspected the crash was the result of some equipment failure.[84]

In response to the Baker/Beazley accident, the Air Board amended the Air Regulations in December 1920.

Ernest Rogers, like his brother Blythe, had the vision to support and invest in aviation development. CITY OF VANCOUVER ARCHIVES. 2011-092.1593

No air pilot of any flying machine shall unless he is alone or has the written permission of his passenger, permit to cause such flying machine to spin, roll, loop, or execute any other evolution involving unnecessary risk.[85]

Had these early aviators tried too much, expected too much? Could commercial aviation be more than just a show of stunting pilots? In 1920, perhaps too much was hoped for, given the aircraft available, the ground infrastructure, the state of pilot training, and lack of civilian experience. Certainly, those with a little foresight and imagination could see what was possible but could not yet realize it. It was early days in the adoption of the new technology for civilian use.

Some, of course, kept trying. Donald MacLaren left the Air Board and, in 1925, became a partner in Pacific Airways Ltd., with one Curtiss JN-4. His partner was Ernest Rogers, who was keeping up the tradition started by his brother Blythe of financing aviation in BC. MacLaren had more success—and luck—than George Trim. Pacific Airways was later bought by Western Airways, which in turn became part of Canadian Airways. When Trans-Canada Air Lines (later Air Canada) was formed in 1937, MacLaren was the first person hired. His role in the development of commercial aviation in Canada was recognized when he was inducted into the Canadian Aviation Hall of Fame.[86]

Godfrey and Trim in the Royal Canadian Air Force

It's not quite true to say that Trim disappeared from the newspapers. In June 1922, Trim is reported as working with Donald MacLaren to produce an air show to raise funds for children's playgrounds.[87] In September 1922, Superintendent MacLaurin of the Air Board was himself killed when his plane crashed into English Bay in Vancouver. Among the pallbearers at his funeral were Captain Trim and Captain Hoy. MacLaurin's replacement at Jericho Beach was Earl Godfrey.

In 1921, Earl Godfrey also tried the aviation business, but in 1922 he was back in the air force. VANCOUVER PROVINCE, 11 JUNE 1921. P28

In March 1924, the federal government, adapting to circumstances and lessons learned, separated civil and military aviation. Godfrey was involved in the creation of the Royal Canadian Air Force, which came into existence on 1 April. It was a small force, with 68 officers and 307 airmen. It would really be a base support system used to give reserves their annual training and provide a small professional corps if expansion were ever needed. Godfrey became a squadron leader and stayed in command at Jericho. He enthusiastically said of the new air force,

> The RCAF is the only military organization in Canada which is partially self-supporting. In fact, it is the only air force in the world which contributes to its upkeep by operation on a repayment basis for governmental departments. That is why its operation can be increased.[88]

One of the first things that Godfrey did was take on several new pilots, and George Trim was one of them. Captain Trim was attested and sworn in personally by Godfrey, but his old friend and commander did not keep George in Vancouver. Trim was sent to Camp Borden in Ontario.

So, after the excitement and disappointment of 1919 and 1920, Trim was back teaching pilots, this time in Avro 504s, which he had flown with the RAF in England. We can only guess at life on the flat windswept plain of Camp Borden. At least Toronto was close by. Soon, however, Trim was sent to England and the RAF's Central Flying School. RAF records are sketchy, but he was there in 1926.[89] As with peacetime life at Camp Borden, it was probably boring, but it was flying.

Earl Godfrey—One of the First

The 1920s and 1930s were the decades of flying firsts, and some of those who performed a first became famous—for example, Alcock and Brown, Amelia Earhart, or Charles Lindbergh. One of these firsts was in 1926 when J. Dalzell McKee and Major Earl Godfrey made a flight across Canada in a Douglas MO-2B seaplane. It was made in thirty-four hours and forty-one minutes flying time.

Godfrey described the possibilities that the flight revealed:

> The route we followed, with few variations, would be suitable for a transcontinental air service. But it would be considerably short- ened by the use of a three engined machine which would eliminate any chance of a forced landing and make it possible to cut across overland in some districts where we followed waterways. Such a machine would also make the trip absolutely safe through the mountains, where most of the danger is to be expected.[90]

McKee donated a trophy, the Trans-Canada Trophy, to be awarded annually to a person who advanced the cause of Canadian aviation. It is now commonly called the McKee Trophy, so named in his honour after he was killed in an air accident while getting ready to try another "first" flight with Godfrey, this time from Montreal to the Yukon, then to Vancouver.

Godfrey's career in "firsts" continued when in September 1928, he carried the first official trans-Canada airmail from Ottawa to Vancouver,[91] a distance of 5,150 kilometres (3,200 miles) covered in 36 hours of flying but spread over three days with six stops along the way for fuel or rest.

Godfrey clearly loved flying as much as Trim and MacLaren but took the path of a career in the air force. In the lean years of the 1930s, with government budgets cut to the bone, he helped keep the

Godfrey got a full page of coverage in the Vancouver *Sunday Province Magazine* for the cross-Canada flight. McKee was not mentioned. Despite Canadian winters, seaplanes were still seriously considered for use in scheduled flights for many years to come. ORIGINALLY PUBLISHED IN THE VANCOUVER SUNDAY PROVINCE MAGAZINE, 8 OCTOBER 1926. A DIVISION OF POSTMEDIA NETWORK, INC.

Air Vice-Marshal Godfrey, centre, inspecting airmen in Newfoundland during the Second World War. CANADA DEPARTMENT OF NATIONAL DEFENCE / LIBRARY AND ARCHIVES CANADA / PA-114774

RCAF going. He was sent to England to take the RAF staff course for higher officers. His evaluation observed that he was not a man for details but was a very good leader.[92] In the Second World War he rose to the high rank of air vice-marshal. While he was inspecting a base, he flew out as a gunner on an anti-submarine patrol and got to fire his machine gun at a U-boat. This gave him the distinction of being the most senior RCAF officer to engage the enemy during the war.

In 1944, Godfrey was due to retire but did not want to in the middle of a war. He approached General Andrew McNaughton, the Minister of National Defence, for an extension of his service. The two men had known each other for decades. McNaughton refused to intervene, fearing a charge of favouritism.[93] Godfrey was very annoyed an decided to enter politics, seek the nomination of the

Co-operative Commonwealth Federation (CCF) Party, and run against McNaughton.

Prime Minister Mackenzie King had selected General McNaughton to be Minister of Defence. But McNaughton needed a seat in the House of Commons if he was to enter King's Liberal government. The Liberal Party found a safe seat and a by-election was called. It was widely covered in the press across Canada because of McNaughton's presence. The CCF must have been delighted to get such a high-profile candidate to run against him. In the vote, McNaughton unexpectedly lost to the Conservative candidate. Godfrey's presence as a CCF candidate split the left-centre vote and prevented McNaughton from gaining a seat in the House of Commons.

Godfrey was awarded the McKee Trophy in 1977 and inducted into the Canadian Aviation Hall of Fame in 1978.

The Flying Clubs—Reviving the Dream

The number of aviation companies and the number of flights declined in the early 1920s despite the best efforts of people like Trim, MacLaren, and others who dreamed of flying. The machines available were not up to the tasks of civilian aviation. The costs of new machines and infrastructure were unknown but definitely high. Spectacular accidents continued despite the best efforts of the Air Board to bring order to flying. Even the world-famous Billy Bishop could not make a go of it. Bishop-Barker Aeroplanes made a start with passenger service and did some barnstorming. They tried air freight too, but the company dissolved in 1921 after Bishop was injured in a crash. Even the big names could not succeed.

The litany of problems continued. In 1926, there were only fourteen registered aviation companies, with forty-four licensed aircraft. No cross-country scheduled airlines were possible without airports. There were no flight schools, so there was a shortage of pilots, with only seventy-two licensed civilian pilots in 1927.[94] How could the dreams of flying, so common in 1919 and 1920, be realized?

Supporters of aviation looked to Britain, and the idea of flying clubs. The plan was to start at the bottom, with local clubs and local enthusiasts funded by the government. With more local aerodromes and private pilots, it was hoped to prime the system.

Canada adopted the British model. Government aid was dependent on a community,

1. Starting a flying club;

2. Building a landing field, hangar, and workshop;

3. Hiring an instructor and a mechanic; and

4. Having ten licensed pilots as members and enrolling thirty students.

To support this local initiative, the federal government would supply two aircraft, and one more to match one bought by the club, to a total of four. The club would also get one hundred dollars for every pupil who got a licence. Given the views on government aid at that period in history, this was generous, and farsighted. The movement was greeted enthusiastically across Canada. Fifteen clubs were formed in 1928 with 2,400 members.[95]

A New Life in Montreal

In 1927, George Trim left the RCAF and began a new life in Montreal. He may have reached a promotion ceiling, or it might have been his eyesight. A photo two years later shows him with stylish spectacles. In October and November, he was a founding member of the Montreal Light Aeroplane Club and elected to its board of directors.[96] In January and February 1928, on behalf of the flying club, he gave a series of talks at McGill University about flying,

The famous de Havilland Moth was commonly used by flying clubs in Canada and the United Kingdom. This Moth was owned by the Montreal Light Aeroplane Club in 1933 and would likely have been flown by George Trim.

A. EDWARD HILL / LIBRARY AND ARCHIVES CANADA / PA-070862

which, as reported in the McGill student paper, were quite technical and detailed.

> Mr. Trim then proceeded to describe steep turns of more than 45 degrees. In these cases, the stick is pulled back sharply. The speaker also described how to get into and out of a spin.[97]

In the 1928 Civil Aviation report of licensed commercial pilots, Trim is listed with an address at 2050 Bleary Street, Montreal. This appears to have been a commercial property, so it was probably his business address, although what business he was with is not stated.

As an active member of the Montreal Light Aeroplane Club, Trim appears in press reports throughout 1928. The club applied for the aid provided by the government. It had 161 flying members and the required buildings and employees at the new flying field at St. Hubert. The chief instructor was Captain F.G.M. Sparks, helped on weekends by Captain Trim and two other volunteers. Captain Trim was also listed among twenty-three members who took a refresher course. The Montreal club was given two DH Moth aircraft; it bought another and was, therefore, given a fourth plane.

When the Granby Flying Club opened as Quebec's second flying club in the summer of 1928, Colonel James L. Ralston, the Minister of National Defence, made the presentation of the government aircraft. Ralston's department was in charge of promoting the flying club movement and supplying the aircraft. In his speech, Ralston said, "It is remarkable to think that thirty-five thousand people flew in Canada last year." He was impressed with the high number.

The *Montreal Gazette* covered the ceremony and reported:

> Captain G.K. Trim, a director of the Montreal Light Aeroplane Club, a member of the Granby Aeroclub, and an instructor of considerable ability, piloted one of the new Granby machines, taking Frank S. McGill, a director of both the Montreal and Granby clubs as a passenger.[98]

Flying was still a dangerous activity. Just weeks after the Granby club opened with great ceremony, Captain Harold Nase, chief flying instructor of the club, was killed when his Moth aircraft stalled on takeoff.[99]

Still single and still an accomplished flyer, Trim was not deterred by the danger of flying. On 2 October 1928, he flew in an air race at St. Hubert that was held to celebrate the inauguration of airmail service between Canada and the United States, and the first daily airmail flight between Montreal and Toronto. It was just after Earl Godfrey had made the first official airmail flight across Canada. The *Gazette* said that Trim raced as a representative of the Continental Aero Corporation, an American maker of aero engines and light aircraft.[100]

Was it possible that the prospects of 1919 might, at last, be met?

In 1929, Trim married Kathleen Hughes of Toronto, and the marriage licence gives his occupation as manufacturer. That might explain the Bleary Street business address, as would his later being reported as president of Trim Industries.

In addition to being a member of the flying clubs, Trim bought his own plane in July 1929—a DH 60 Moth on floats. Unfortunately, it was wrecked beyond repair while being towed to a seaplane base shortly after the purchase.[101] This piece of bad luck did not stop him from being involved in aviation safety. He was invited by the Province of Quebec Safety League to be a member of its aeroplane safety committee. The American publication *Aviation Week* described the purpose of this league:

> To promote safety principles of aviation by fostering a sense of responsibility among airplane manufacturers and pilots... and to investigate and explain to the public the causes of accidents.

"Capt. George K. Trim, late of the RFC, RAF, and RCAF," was listed as an officer of the league.[102]

The Monocoupe was a small aircraft designed for private flyers. Trim had no chance to win against larger aircraft, but he may have been acting as a salesman in this instance. This photo from 1928 shows a Monocoupe in the RCAF, where Trim may have flown it. CANADA DEPARTMENT OF NATIONAL DEFENCE / LIBRARY AND ARCHIVES CANADA / PA-062437

George Trim (left) and F.S. Molson, 6 October 1929. Both were members of the Montreal Racquets Club, serving as Directors. In a short time, Trim had developed important connections, Molson being from THE Montreal Mol-sons. CANADA DEPARTMENT OF NATIONAL DEFENCE / LIBRARY AND ARCHIVES CANADA / PA-062700

Clearly at age thirty-five, he was an experienced and respected flyer. In December 1929, he gave a radio address on air safety. The lessons that Trim had learned in 1920 are evident in his remarks.

We want the public to be air-minded in every sense of the word, and we want them to know all the Canadian Air Rules and Regulations governing aircraft, pilots and air mechanics; also to remember that the machine must be carefully inspected before each flight, to know the maximum load the machine is allowed to carry...

We hope that next year will see the inauguration of radio beacons on some commercial air routes in Canada. Radio direction for mail routes makes it possible to fly through fog, at present the greatest danger to air travel. On radio equipped airways it is possible for the pilot to keep on his exact course in complete darkness.

The Aviation Committee of the Province of Quebec Safety League hopes for the strictest enforcement of regulations for the inspection of airplanes and engines before each flight. It insists that pilots pass a rigid examination in navigation and radios; that all routes be marked by radio beacons, and that there shall be emergency landing fields along each air route in case of forced landings and that there will be a greater number of equipped airports throughout Canada.

Everything possible is being done by the Quebec Safety League, with the co-operation of all concerned to show that with proper inspection of pilots, mechanics, machines and engines and with the use of all safety devices, flying is a safe means of transportation.[103]

A prolonged period of quiet then descends—at least for Trim in the press. He presumably was active with these new flying connections in Quebec. He continued to promote air mindedness, for example by providing the Captain George Trim Trophy to the Model Aircraft League of Canada, for annual presentation to a winning model club.[104] This was not insignificant, as modelling was seen as an important way to promote aviation with youth.[105] But that was all of Trim in the press for years.

The Labrador Air Crash

The publication of the following note was sensational and brought to a close the saga of a crash and subsequent search operation in remote Labrador in 1939-40. The urgency and the concern for notification of families is poignant.

This $180 is the money of three dying men and belongs to you. Go at once to the nearest wireless or telegraph office and report to the

DH89 Rapide. The plane owned by Quebec Airways was similar. The Labrador
plane was recovered and remained in service until 1949. CANADA DEPART-
MENT OF NATIONAL DEFENCE / LIBRARY AND ARCHIVES CANADA / PA-063108

government that you have found our bodies and the plane CF-BND lost in September on a trip to Northeast River.

The plane rests safely on the shore of a large lake northwest of here about two miles. Have the message sent to the government at once. Be sure and report at once.

Any other expense you have will be paid to you. Come back here at once and guard our bodies. And the plane and keep faithfully the box containing our letters to our family.

An airplane will come to take us to Montreal.

Guard everything well. You will be paid for your work. Show this to the operator. Relay the news at once. Do this Christian work at once for the sake of our families.

J.C. Cote, G.H. Davidson, Joseph Fecteau.

George Trim flew to Labrador and brought back the bodies and the diary of G.H. Davidson.

A Sensational Story

A Rapide aircraft owned by Quebec Airways was hired by George H. Davidson to fly into remote Labrador to make a timber survey. They set out on 10 September 1939. Davidson was the secretary treasurer of Macfarlane, Son & Hodgson Ltd., an Ottawa paper company. With Davidson was Joseph C. Cote, a paper mill manager, and Joseph Fecteau, pilot for Quebec Airways. In bad weather, the plane ran out of fuel and made a safe landing on a lake, and the three men found shelter in a nearby trapper's cabin. They had a radio from the plane and sent out messages twice a day, but the radio did not have the range to be heard in that wilderness.

In Montreal, Davidson's family became more and more desperate for news and, on 20 September, called on their friend George

Trim to help organize a search. At first Quebec Airways was reluctant to launch a search, believing the plane was just delayed, but Davidson's father-in-law, C.H. MacFarlane, offered to pay some of the expenses. At Trim's urging, Quebec Airways sent one plane, the only available. Two days later five more planes had been chartered, but then bad weather grounded them. Trim was not happy with the aircraft being used as they did not have the range needed. Quebec Airways could not find any in the whole of Canada that were available for charter. The RCAF had none of its long-range planes ready. There was no formal search and rescue system. Trim joined the search in a plane piloted by Michael DeBlicquy, general manager of Quebec Airways.

On 20 October, the search was called off because of winter weather. The only hope was that the men, if still alive, might be able to reach settlements on the coast of Labrador.

In late February 1940, the trapper who owned the cabin where the men died found their bodies and notified authorities. On 5 March the news broke across Canada.[105] The bodies were taken by dogsled to Hopedale, Labrador. Acting at the request of the Davidson family, George Trim made the journey on a Quebec Airways flight piloted by Bill Ressignier. It took twelve days in ice, fog, and blizzard. Trim described their arrival.

> We saw a lighthouse and an Eskimo [Inuit] home. We were 17 miles from Hopedale where the Eskimos had marked out runways on the ice in Hopedale Bay.[107]

Trim made the journey to the cabin and found two tiny rooms, two bunks, a table, and a stove. The Rapide airplane was found in good shape, but with no fuel.

A coroner's inquest was immediately held, and the story went out on the news wires. The letters and diaries showed that the men had been alive as late as 17 December, almost three months after they took shelter in the trapper's cabin. They had died of starvation and cold. Two bodies were found in the bunks, one on the floor. The diaries and letters left by the men began to be released a few days after the inquest found that the deaths were by accident. The story caused a sensation and was reported around the world.

Joseph C. Cote

Last letters, dated November 22 to 26.

> I visited a few traps some yards from here. I walked like an old man with a cane. If we have not had help by Sunday, we will render our account to the Supreme Judge.
>
> After 3 days of nothing but water I was able to get up. I went to the traps. As usual they were empty.
>
> The others kept the fire going all night otherwise we could not have escaped death. It will only delay the end. It will be here soon.
>
> My Eva and Claude [son] I leave you for eternity with resignation and unshaken faith. A thousand kisses.[108]

Joseph Fecteau, pilot

> November 3. One day I was able to go hunting and shot 60 partridges and a porcupine which have prolonged our days by at least 3 weeks, and we are gathering clams.
>
> November 17. Providence has come to our aid. A porcupine and a weasel passed our camp no more than 2 feet away. All is in God's hands.
>
> Relatives and friends, I am obliged to leave you through death, a death which is the saddest I could imagine. Since our own sad

and tragic situation first arose there has always been before us a small ray of hope which faded from day to day.

  December 9. My wife, I probably will die in a very short while.[109]

What a very sad and heart-rending story.

A second official investigation into how the aircraft came to be lost was conducted by the Department of Transport. It concluded, on 14 May 1940, that the men had died after an accident caused by the faulty navigation of the pilot, who was ill.[110] The machine was found to be new, entirely airworthy, and intact when recovered, apart from the lack of gas. The report stated that Fecteau had admitted in his letters to having "lost command of his faculties" during the trip. No breach of air regulations was found, but in future pilots were advised to carry a fish net, to consult a physician at the first sign of illness, and to leave aircraft that had been forced to land in a conspicuous place.[111]

The Courts

The widows of Davidson and Cote were understandably not satisfied and sued Quebec Airways for $110,000. The trial was held in Montreal in March 1942.

The lawyers for the widows presented their evidence and brought in expert witnesses, including George Trim. Among the most explosive allegations were those made by Davidson himself in his diary. He especially complained about a last-minute change of pilots. Davidson said, "I would never have made a move from Montreal had I been told. Deceit, Deception."[112]

The radio also received special attention. In his diary, Davidson said that they had sent out radio messages twice a day for six weeks, but never heard anything. One expert witness stated that it had a range of about a mile and was worse than useless.

The *Ottawa Journal* carried coverage of the trial.

George Trim, a pilot and friend of Davidson, testified today he had advised Davidson to make the trip on the basis of assurance that a radio would be carried, and the pilot would be either Michael De Blicquy or Joseph Forrester. Trim said he would have advised Davidson to see another company if he had known Fecteau was to pilot the plane because "you need not only flying experience, but you need a man who can size up a situation."[113]

The Quebec Airways defence was that there was an accident. They too summoned expert witnesses about the radio and pointed out that there was no regulation requiring that a plane carry one. They also argued that there had been no agreement about who should fly the charter.

To counter George Trim as an expert witness, the defence called upon one of the most famous pilots in Canada. It is safe to say that C.H. "Punch" Dickins is one of the most famous of all Canadian aviators. He was a pilot with the RAF in 1918 and although flying bombers, also became an ace, shooting down seven enemy aircraft. He was awarded the Distinguished Flying Cross for bravery. After the war he became one of the most famous bush pilots of the 1920s and logged over 1.6 million kilometres flying in the north. He was awarded the McKee Trophy in 1928 for his northern flying and made an officer of the Order of the British Empire in 1935. He was a formidable witness.

Punch Dickins testified that he had found the logbook of pilot Fecteau to be in good order and found no evidence of faulty navigation. The *Montreal Gazette* reported that Dickins said, "In that territory the best pilot was likely to get lost. He would then direct his course according to his best judgement. There was no manifest error in the course." He also said that he had used the same radio in bush flying in Northern Canada for Canadian Airways and "it gave useful service."[114]

The trial was held before a judge, who was not sufficiently impressed by Punch Dickins and found for the plaintiffs. He awarded Mrs. Davidson and her daughters $41,000 and Mrs. Cote was awarded $13,000. In his finding the judge pointed out the main factors in his decision:

- The substitution of an incompetent pilot
- A faulty fuel gauge on the plane
- A poor radio
- Quebec Airways failing to arrange a radio listening watch.

If George Trim had sought redemption after his role in Beazley's death in 1920, it might have been this.

A Fulfilling and Successful Life

There is no evidence that George Trim played a further public role in aviation. He was a businessman and involved in aviation through the Trim Companies. His name appears in the press as a member of the board of governors of Montreal General Hospital. In the 1950s, he became vice-president of MacFarlane, Son & Hodgson. Trim retired from business in 1961. Social pages show that he often holidayed abroad with his wife, and they moved to Magog, Quebec. After his wife died suddenly while they were on vacation in Switzerland in 1973, Trim moved back to British Columbia, buying a house in Oak Bay on Vancouver Island. When he died there in September 1982, at the age of 87, his obituary called him a pioneer of aviation. That he was.

An appropriate epitaph for George Trim is a description of the air show he performed in Granby at the opening of the flying club there. It is a reminder of both his skill as a pilot and his devotion to flying, and hearkens back to when he was a newly returned veteran pilot of 1919.

George Trim gave a wonderful exhibition of stunt flying, demonstrating an ease of control that sent his airplane through every conceivable evolution. With the sun glinting on its silver wings the machine hovered over the heads of spectators, dived low and zoomed up in a perpendicular climb. The feathered members of the species were absent from the aerodrome on Saturday, being entirely outclassed by the man-made bird cars. [115]

ACKNOWLEDGEMENTS

I OWE A GREAT debt of gratitude to people who have close family connections to the airmen in this book. James Thayer of Seattle is a first cousin twice removed of Osborne Orr. His great grand-mother was Caroline Orr's sister Harriet (standing, right, in the family photo). Jim has generously and enthusiastically made available family photos and history for the story of Osborne Orr. Jim, an accomplished author and teacher of writing, also read an early draft of Part Two, and his comments are treasured. Jim and his sister Connie Thayer repatriated Orr's DFC and service medals to Canada in the care of the Vancouver Island Military Museum. Finding the medals of a Canadian ace in 2021 was a special moment. Doreen O'Keefe of Courtenay, BC, is the daughter of Oliver Gagnier from Part One. She provided family photos and stories that reveal the amazing character of her father. Mike Fall provided photos and family history about his father, Joseph Fall, one of the great aces of the war. It has been a great privilege to deal with James, Doreen, and Mike. A century melted away.

My colleagues at the Vancouver Island Military Museum deserve special mention. Volunteers all, they spend innumerable hours preserving the past. Roger Bird and Brian McFadden especially made sure that Osborne Orr has been properly commemorated in the city of his birth.

Archivists and librarians protect and preserve our heritage. The staff at Archival and Special Collections, University of Guelph seem to have had as much joy in finding materials for this book as I did. Emilie Vandal, Chief Archivist, Directorate of History and Heritage, Department of National Defence did not hesitate to track down an important photo, ably helped by her predecessor Mathias Joost. What dedication. Also, thanks to the staff of the Canadian War Museum, the RAF Museum, the History Museum of Canada, the Imperial War Museum, BC Archives, and University of British Columbia Archives. The following archivists deserve special mention for helping in the search for the lost records of service in Canada of Canadians who joined the Imperial Royal Flying Corps:

- Mary Munk, Library and Archives Canada;

- Michael Little, National Archives, UK;

- Christina Parsons, Canadian War Museum;

- Emilie Vandal, Directorate of History and Heritage, Department of National Defence;

- Jennifer Dunn, National Air Force Museum of Canada;

- Megan Strain, City of Toronto Archives;

- Amanda Hill, Community Archives of Belleville and Hastings County; and

- Katherine Browne, Flying Heritage and Combat Armor Museum, Seattle.

Alec MacInnes, principal, and the staff of Britannia Secondary School in Vancouver keep alive the memory of Osborne Orr and all the graduates of the school who died in service of their country. Henk Uitslag of the Netherlands provided one of his aviation art paintings for use in the book. It was a pleasure to deal with him.

Andrew Dawrant and the volunteers of the Royal Aero Club have worked hard to provide photos for this book and have made their precious records available to all researchers. Their efforts are greatly appreciated.

My great strength and support during the writing of this book has been my wife, Jill. Her eagle eye for spelling and grammar and her general sense were essential, and her patience, as always, is remarkable.

ENDNOTES

Part One: Youth Ascending

1 William Avery Bishop. *Winged Warfare* (Toronto: McClelland, Goodchild, and Stewart Publishers, 1918), from the original preface.

2 Glen C. Phillips. *The Ontario Photographer List, Vol. II* (London, ON: Iron Gate Publishing. London, ON, 1987); and David V. Tinder. *Directory of Early Michigan Photographers* (Ann Arbor: University of Michigan Clements Library, 2013).

3 Ronald Gadd. *Combat Stress Reactions and Morale in RFC/RAF Aircrew 1914-1918* (PhD Thesis. University of Wolverhampton, 2020).

4 S.F. Wise. *Canadian Airmen and the First World War* (Toronto: University of Toronto Press, 1980), 4, 8, 10, 12-13.

5 Glenn H. Curtiss and Augustus Post. *The Curtiss Aviation Book* (New York: Frederick A. Stokes Co., 1912), 42-43.

6 Deposition by J.A.D. McCurdy, April 9, 1920. MSS1268. Library of Congress. Washington. www.loc.gov/resource/magbell.14410301

7 Laurence Surtees. "Bell, Alexander Graham," *Dictionary of Canadian Biography,* vol. 15 (University of Toronto/Universite Laval, 2005).

8 S.F. Wise. *Canadian Airmen and the First World War* (Toronto: University of Toronto Press, 1980), 17-18.

9 Deposition by J.A.D. McCurdy, April 9, 1920. MSS1268. Library of Congress. Washington. www.loc.gov/resource/magbell.14410301

10 Wise. *Canadian Airmen and the First World War*, 31.

11 Ibid., 30.

12 Ibid., 192.

13 Ibid., 39.

14 *Calgary Herald.* 6 November 1915. 14.

15 Wise. *Canadian Airmen and the First World War*, 33.

16 Ibid., 41–42.

17 The National Archives of the UK. ADM 273/7/166. Index No. 37538.

18 Ibid.

19 Personnel Records of the First World War. Library and Archives Canada. R.G. 150. Accession 1992/93 Box 7040-15 Item 161718.

20 *Eaton's Goes to War*. Archives of Ontario.

21 The National Archives of the UK, AIR 76/324/198, Image 602.

22 The identification of Briggs, Hunter, and King as mechanics is from an undated newspaper clipping provided to the author by Doreen Gagnier O'Keefe, daughter of student O.J. Gagnier in the photo. The clipping shows a version of the group portrait, with accompanying identifications that correspond to those written on the group photo used here, along with an explanation of the Curtiss operations. Mrs. O'Keefe's clipping is undoubtedly contemporary with the group photo used here.

23 National Archives of the UK. Air 76/245/57.

24 National Archives of the UK. Air 76/277/5.

25 Curtiss School of Aviation fonds. Daily Flying Records—May, June, July 1916. MG28 III Vol 1. Library and Archives Canada.

26 David Hobbs. *The Royal Navy's Air Service in the Great War* (Barnsley, Yorkshire: Seaforth Publishing, 2017), 541.

27 J. Playford Hales letter to Ernest Hales. Archives and Special Collections, University of Guelph. XR1 MS A519 (6).

28 National Archives of the UK, ADM 273/10/126. Index No. 38388.

29 Mike Westrop. *A History of No. 6 Squadron, Royal Naval Air Service* (Artglen, PA: Schiffer Publishing), 29.

30 Family history provided in January 2021 by Doreen O'Keefe, daughter of Oliver Gagnier.

31 Doreen Gagnier O'Keefe. Correspondence with author, January 2020.

32 Maurice Baring. *Flying Corps Headquarters 1914–1918* (London: G. Bell and Sons, 1920).

33 Westrop. *A History of No. 6 Squadron, Royal Naval Air Service*.

34 Ibid., 221.

35 Arthur Gould Lee. *No Parachute* (London: Grub Street, 2013), 48.

36 Westrop. *A History of No. 6 Squadron, Royal Naval Air Service*, 67.

37 Ibid., 67–68.

38 National Archives of the UK, ADM 273/10/126. Index No. 38388.

39 National Archives of the UK, Air 76/174/51.

40 Doreen Gagnier O'Keefe. Correspondence with author, January 2020.

41 Stewart K. Taylor. "Naval's Bad Boy: FSL Arthur McBurney Walton, A Flight, 6 Squadron RNAS 1917." *Cross and Cockade International* 38/3 2007: 168–170.

42 National Archives of the UK, ADM 273/10/128.

43 Ibid.

44 Mayo Clinic. mayoclinic.org

45 Nick Bartlett. *In the Teeth of the Wind: Memoirs of the Royal Naval Air Service in the First World War* (London: Lee Cooper Publishers, 2013), 272.

46 Jon Guttmann. *Naval Aces of World War I, Part I* (Oxford: Osprey Publishing, 2011), 14.

47 Westrop. *A History of No. 6 Squadron, Royal Naval Air Service*, 84.

48 Ronald Gadd. *Combat Stress Reactions and Morale in RFC/RAF Aircrew 1914–1918*. PhD Thesis. University of Wolverhampton, 2020. See Chapter One, page 38 ("Aircrew Morale," "Group Effectiveness"), page 39 ("Group Coherence "), and page 42 ("Fear").

49 National Archives of the UK. Knight: ADM 273/10/140, McCrudden, ADM 273/10/97, McDonald ADM 273/10/127.

50 Graham Pitchfork. *Forever Vigilant: Naval 8/208 Squadron RAF. A Century of Service from 1916 to 2016* (London: Grub Street Publishing, 2016), 138.

51 Ibid., 74.

52 McCrudden. Casualty Report. www.naval8-208-association.com/WWI/RollofHonourMcCrudden.html.

53 National Archives of the UK. Knight: ADM 273/10/140, Air 76/279/163.

54 Jocelyn Gillis. 8 May 1918. "Lieutenant Roderick McDonald." *Antigonish Cenotaph Project, Antigonish Heritage Museum.* 2008. https://antigonishcenotaphproject.wordpress.com/2018/05/08/may-8-1918-lieutenant-roderick-macdonald/.

55 National Archives of the UK. McDonald ADM 273/10/127.

56 Pitchfork. *Forever Vigilant*, 107.

57 Christopher Cole ed. *Royal Air Force Communiques 1918* (London: Tom Donovan Publishers, 1990), 41.

58 Douglas Marr. "Naval 8 WWI," *Naval 8-208 Squadron History*: 148. www.naval8-208-association.com.

59 National Archives of the UK. Ellis. ADM273/10/55.

60 Letter reproduced in Allan D. Bennett. *Captain Roy Brown: A True Story of the Great War, 1914–1918* (New York: Brick Tower Press. 2012, and ibooks 2014).

61 Paul Dickson. "Stinson, Marion Elizabeth (Crerar)" *Dictionary of Canadian Biography, vol. 14* (University of Toronto/Universite Laval, 1998). www.biographi.ca/en/bio/stinson_marion_elizabeth_14E.html.

62 M.B. Wansbrough. *Echoes That Remain: Highfield School History* (Hamilton: Highfield- Strathallan College, 2001), 33.

63 National Archives of the UK. Crerar. Air 76/112/149.

64 Toronto *Star*. 9 August 1917.

65 See Commonwealth War Graves Commission, Malcolm Charlton Crerar. Headstone directions from Lt. Col. H.D.G. Crerar. www.cwgc.org/find-records/find-war-dead/casualty-details/645526/MALCOLM%20CHARLTON%20CRERAR/.

66 National Archives of the UK. Blyth. ADM 273/10/47.

67 Commonwealth War Graves Commission. www.cwgc.org/find-records/find-war-dead/casualty-details/103030/R%20A%20BLYTH/.

68 Wise. *Canadian Airmen and the First World War,* 172.

69 National Archives of the UK. J.R. Allan. ADM 273/10/46 and AIR 76/5/48.

70 National Archives of the UK. Capt. Paul Bewsher. ADM 273/16/99.

71 S.K. Taylor. "John Roy Allan – Handley-Page Pilot," *The Journal of the Canadian Aviation Historical Society.* Vol. 34, No. 3, Winter 1996: 137.

72 Paul Bewsher. *Green Balls: The Adventures of a Night Bomber* (London: William Black and Sons, 1919), 286–87.

73 National Archives of the UK. Hales. ADM 273/10/300.

74 J. Playford Hales letter to Ernest Hales, 27 Feb. 1918. Archives and Special Collections, University of Guelph. XR1 MS A519.

75 National Archives of the UK. Hales. Air/76/202.

76 Wise. *Canadian Airmen and the First World War,* 550.

77 J. Playford Hales letter to Jean and Ernest Hales, 15 August 1918. Archives and Special Collections, University of Guelph. XR1 MS A519.

78 RAF Casualty Card. www.rafmuseumstoryvault.org.uk/archive/7000245767-hales-j.p.-john-playford.

79 "Robert Leckie," *100 Stories*. Library and Archives Canada. www.bac-lac.gc.ca/eng/discover/military-heritage/first-world-war/100-stories/Pages/leckie.aspx.

80 "Flying Boats Over the North Sea," RAF Museum. www.rafmuseum.org.uk/blog/flying-boats-over-the-north-sea/.

81 Air Marshal Robert Leckie. www.rcafassociation.ca/advocacy/airpower-advocacy-committee/commanders-canadas-air-force/air-marshal-robert-leckie/.

82 Lyndsay Rosenthal. "New Battlegrounds: Treating VD in Belgium and Germany, 1918–19," in *Canada 1919: A Nation Shaped by War*, eds. Tim Cook and J.L Granatstein (Vancouver: UBC Press, 2020), 57.

83 "Major military awards of World War I: VC to MID," *The Gazette*. London. www.thegazette.co.uk/awards-and-accreditation/medals.

84 Curtiss School of Aviation fonds. Daily Flying Records – May, June, July, August 1916. MG28 III Vol 1. Library and Archives Canada.

85 Wise. *Canadian Airmen and the First World War*, 176, 250.

86 National Archives of the UK. ADM 273/12/29.

87 National Archives of the UK. ADM 273/10/301.

88 National Archives of the UK. ADM 273/10/208.

89 *McGill Honour Roll 1914–18* (Montreal: McGill University, 1926).

90 National Archives of the UK. A.C. Reid. Air/76/421/42. *The London Gazette*, 2 November 1918.

91 207 Squadron Royal Air Force History: World War I. www.207squadron.rafinfo.org.uk.

92 National Archives of the UK. ADM 273/10/45.

93 Wise. *Canadian Airmen and the First World War*, 304.

94 *London Gazette*, 17 November 1917.

95 See photos in S.K. Taylor. "John Roy Allan – Handley-Page Pilot," *The Journal of the Canadian Aviation Historical Society*. Vol. 34, No. 3, Winter 1996.

96 Wise. *Canadian Airmen and the First World War*, 293, 302, 304, 311.

97 National Archives of the UK. Johnson. ADM 273/10/45.

98 Sampson J. Goodfellow. *One Lucky Devil: The First World War Memoirs of Sampson J. Goodfellow*, ed. Edward Willett (Regina: Shadowpaw Press, 2018), 132.

99 National Archives of the UK. Eckardt. AIR 76/145/195, AIR 76/145/189, AIR 76/145/211.

100 Harold Price. "Diary," in *A Rattle of Pebbles: The First World War Diaries of Two Canadian Airmen*, ed. Brereton Greenhous (Ottawa: Canadian Government Publication Centre, 1997), 163.

101 Alan Sullivan. *Aviation in Canada, 1917-1918* (Toronto: Rous and Mann, 1919), 224.

102 National Archives of the UK. ADM 273/10/238, AIR 76/334/223.

103 Bewsher. *Green Balls*, 287.

Part Two: Youth Lost

1   Ibid., 31.
2   John MacGavock Grider. *War Birds: Diary of an Unknown Aviator* (College Station, TX: Texas A&M University Press, 1988), 14
3   Wise. *Canadian Airmen and the First World War,* 87.
4   *Austin American.* 3 April 1918.
5   Lester B. Pearson. *Mike: 1897–1948* (Toronto: University of Toronto Press, 2015), xii.
6   James McCudden. *Flying Fury: Five Years in the Royal Flying Corps* (Oxford: Casemate Publishers (Ignition), 2009), 269
7   Kilduff, Peter. *Billy Bishop VC Lone Wolf Hunter: The RAF Ace Re-Examined* (London: Grub Street, 2014), 42.
8   Jackson, Robert. *Britain's Greatest Aircraft* (Oxford: Casemate Publishers, 2007), 2.
9   www.theaerodrome.com/aces/index.php.
10 Desmond Morton. "The Bonus Campaign. 1919–21: Veterans and Campaign for Re-establishment," *Canadian Historical Review.* LXVI, 2, 1983: 54.
11 www.veterans.gc.ca/eng/remembrance/memorials/Canadian-virtual-war-memorial.

Part Three: Youth Transcended

1   Bill C. Kilgrain. *Royal Flying Corps: Training Squadrons in Canada and the USA, 1917–1918* (self-published, 2013), 49.
2   T.S. Ripon and E.G. Manuel. "The Essential Characteristics of Successful and Unsuccessful Aviators, with Special Reference to Temperament," *The Lancet.* September 1918.
3   George K. Trim. Record of Promotions and Appointments.central. bac-lac.gc.ca/.item/?op=pdF&App=CEF&Id=B9785-S033.
4   *Library and Archives Canada.* George Knopp Trim, 20825. The clerk filling out the Attestation Paper misspelled his middle name as Knapp.
5   George K. Trim. Record of Promotions and Appointments. central. bac-lac.gc.ca/.item/?op=pdF&App=CEF&Id=B9785-S033.
6   *National Archives UK,* Air 76. Service file George K Trim, RFC.
7   Geoffrey Wall quoted in Ian Mackersey. *No Empty Chairs: The Short and Heroic Lives of the Young Aviators Who Fought and Died in the First World War* (London: Orion Books, 2012), Chapter 6.

8   Wise. *Canadian Airmen and the First World War,* 87.

9   George K. Trim. Proceedings of Medical Board. 8 September 1916. central.bac-lac.gc.ca/.item/?op=pdF&App=CEF&Id=B9785-S033.

10 George K. Trim. The National Archives. AIR 76/513/27.

11 *Vancouver Daily World.* 8 April 1911, 26 September 1918.

12 *The Province.* 10 December 1910.

13 Godfrey RAF service file – UK National Archives. AIR 76/185/97.

14 *London Gazette.* 26 July 1917.

15 This is especially noted in the memoirs of some surviving pilots. See for example: Arthur Gould Lee. *No Parachute: A Classis Account of the War in the Air in WWI in Letters Written in 1917 by Lieutenant A.S.G. Lee* (London, Grub Street, 2013); Arthur Gould Lee. *Open Cockpit: A Pilot of the Royal Flying Corps* (London: Grub Street, 2012); Also: Lynsey Shaw Cobden. "The Nervous Flyer: Nerves, Flying and the First World War," *British Journal of Military History.* 2018 Feb. 2: 4(2): 121–42.

16 Laura Brandon. "Double Exposure: Photography and the Great War Paintings of Frank Johnston, Arthur Lismer, and Frederick Varley," *RCAR: Revue d'art Canadienne/Canadian Art Review, 39 (2), 14-28.* doi. org/10.7202/1027746ar.

17 Ibid., doi.org/10.7202/1027746ar.

18 B.J. Brinkworth. "On the Early History of Spinning and Spin Research in the UK, Part 1: The Period 1909-1929," *Journal of Aeronautical History.* 2014/03.

19 William Avery Bishop. *Winged Warfare.* ed. Jonathan Reeve (Tunbridge Wells: Spitfire Publishing, 2020).

20 L.A. Strange. *Recollections of an Airman* (Havertown PA: Casemate Publishers, 2016), 148.

21 Tom LeCompte. "The Few, the Brave, the Lucky," *Air and Space Magazine.* July 2008.

22 Elizabeth O'Kiely. *Gentleman Air Ace: the Duncan Bell-Irving Story* (Madeira Park, BC: Harbour Publishing, 1992).

23 Hugh A. Halliday. "Godfrey of the RCAF: Air Force, Part 9," *Legion Magazine.* 1 May 2005. Also, William E. Chajkowsky. *Royal Flying Corps: Borden to Texas to Beamsville* (Cheltenham, ON: Boston Mills Press, 1979).

24 Alan Sullivan. *Aviation in Canada 1917 – 1918* (Toronto: Rous and Mann, 1919).

25 *Montreal Gazette.* 6 May 1919, 9.

26 Ibid.

27 W.A.B. Douglas. *The Creation of a National Air Force: The Official History of the Royal Canadian Air Force, Volume II* (Toronto: University of Toronto Press, 1986), 45–47

28 "The Aerial League of Canada," *The Daily Colonist*. 28 May 1919.

29 *The Province*. 6 May 1920.

30 *Vancouver Daily World*. 22 March 1919.

31 *The Province*. 3 May 1919. *The Vancouver Sun*. 21 July 1919.

32 *The Vancouver Sun*. 21 July 1919.

33 *Vancouver Daily World*. 6 May 1919; *The Province*, 4 June 1919.

34 *Vancouver Daily World*. 10 May 1919.

35 *The Province*. 20 May 1919.

36 *The Province*. 4 June 1919.

37 *Vancouver Daily World*. 23 June 1919.

38 *Winnipeg Tribune*. 26 June 1919.

39 *Edmonton Journal*. 31 May 1919.

40 *The Province*. 2 July 1919.

41 *Victoria Daily Colonist*. 5 July 1919; *The Province*. 5 July and 7 July 1919.

42 *Vancouver Daily World*. 22 July 1919.

43 *Vancouver Sun*. 21 July 1919.

44 *Vancouver Daily World*. 07 08 1919; *Calgary Herald*. 8 August and 13 August 1919.

45 *The Victoria Daily Colonist*. 13 August 1919.

46 *The O.A.C. Review*. Volume 32, No. 1, September 1919; *The Scranton Tribune*, 28 June 1920; *The Chilliwack Progress*, 14 August 1919.

47 *The Victoria Daily Times*. 5 September 1919.

48 *The Province*. 12 July 1981.

49 *The Province*. 4 May 1920.

50 *Nelson Daily News*. 26 September 1919. Quoted in Henry Stevenson, "Planes over the Kootenays," *Journal of the B.C. Historical Federation*. Fall, 1991: 5–6. Clipping at the *Kutne Reader*, www.gregnesteroff. wixsite.com.

51 *Vancouver Daily World*. 01 October 1919.

52 Jonathan F. Vance. *High Flight: Aviation and the Canadian Imagination* (Toronto: Penguin, 2002), 73.

53 *Vancouver Daily World*, 3 Jan 1920; *Vancouver Sun*, 3 January 1920.

54 *Vancouver Daily World*. 19 February 1920.

55 *The Province*, 26 Jan 1920; *The Vancouver Sun*, 16 April 1920.

56 *The Province.* 28 January 1920.

57 *The Province.* 2 February 1920.

58 *The Province.* 30 March 1920 and 2 April 1920; *Vancouver Daily World,* 1 April 1920.

59 *Vancouver Daily World.* 28 April 1920.

60 Kilgrain. *Royal Flying Corps.*

61 Wayne Ralph. *Barker* VC (Toronto: Doubleday Canada, 1998), 185.

62 *The Province.* 30 March 1920.

63 *Vancouver Sun.* 16 April 1920.

64 *The Province.* 28 April 1920.

65 *Vancouver Daily World.* 29 April 1920.

66 *The Province.* 4 May 1920, 9.

67 *The Province.* 14 May 1920, 3.

68 *The Province.* 20 May 1920.

69 *Coroner's Inquisition Report.* BC Archives. GR-0431.12.2.5-Ernest Henry Beazley, 2.

70 *Vancouver Sun.* 25 May 1920, 3.

71 *Vancouver Daily World.* 27 May 1920.

72 *Air 76.* UK National Archives.

73 *American Aeronautics.* 1922 V12: 400.

74 Christopher Shores, Norman Franks, and Russell Guest. *Above the Trenches: A Complete Record of the Fighter Aces and Units of the British Empire Air Forces, 1915-1920* (London: Grub Street, 1990); The Aerodrome. www.theaerodrome.com.

75 *Air Regulations 1920* (Ottawa: Printer to the King's Most Excellent Majesty, 1920). archive.org/details/AirRegulationsCanada1920/mode/2up.

76 *Victoria Daily Times.* 29 May 1920; *Vancouver Daily World.* 3 July 1920.

77 W.A.B. Douglas. *The Creation of a National Air Force. The Official History of the Royal Canadian Air Force.* Volume II (Toronto: University of Toronto Press, 1986), 43.

78 Peter Pigott. *Brace for Impact: Air Crashes and Aviation Safety* (Toronto: Dundurn Press, 2016), Chapter 3.

79 *Victoria Daily Times.* 29 May 1920.

80 *The Province.* 3 July 1920.

81 *Vancouver Daily World.* 6 July 1920.

82 "Popular Aviator Comes to Stay," *Merritt Herald.* 2 July 1920. "Trim Montreal."

83   *Vancouver Daily World.* 19 August 1920.

84   *Vancouver Daily Province.* 19 August 1920, 1.

85   *Victoria Daily Times.* 23 December 1920.

86   Roger Gunn. *Masters of the Air: The Great War Pilots McLeod, McKeever, and MacLaren* (Toronto: Dundurn Press, 2019), 290.

87   *Vancouver Daily World.* 17 June 1922.

88   *The Province.* 25 March 1924.

89   D'Arcy Greig, Norman Franks. *My Golden Flying Years.* Grub Street Press. London, 2011. *RAF Personnel Records*, UK National Archives.

90   Quoted in, Cecil Scott. "By Seaplane Across Canada," *Magazine Section, Vancouver Sunday Province.* 03 October 1926, 37.

91   Canadian Aviation Hall of Fame. www.cahf.ca/CUSTOMPAGES/907/MemberList.cfm?firstLetter=G#87.

92   Hugh A. Halliday. "Godfrey of the RCAF: Air Force, Part 9," *Legion Magazine.* 1 May 2005. legionmagazine.com/en/2005/05/godfrey-of-the-rcaf/.

93   John Swettenham. *McNaughton.* Vol. 3 (Toronto: The Ryerson Press, 1969), 72.

94   "Commercial air pilots engaged in aviation in Canada, 1928." *Report on Civil Aviation and Civil Government – AIR OPERATIONS 1928.* Dominion of Canada, 1928.

95   Wayne C. McNeal. *General Aviation in Canada.* (MA thesis: UBC, 1965). Douglas. *The Creation of a National Air Force,* 83.

96   *Montreal Gazette,* 18 October 1927; *Vancouver Province,* 27 November 1927.

97   "Planes Must Be Inspected for Each Hop," *McGill Daily.* 31 January 1928. "Co-ordination of Controls is Important. G.K. Trim Described Their Use to Aero Club. Spins and Dives." *McGill Daily.* 21 February 1928.

98   *Montreal Gazette.* 18 June 1928, 16.

99   www.aviationsafety.net. 29 August 1928.

100 *Montreal Gazette.* 2 October 1928.

101 www.aviationsafety.net. 27 July 1929.

102 *Aviation Week.* 28 December 1929.

103 "Air Security is Matter of Care," *Montreal Gazette.* 13 December 1929.

104 *Montreal Gazette.* 27 March 1933.

105 Jonathan F. Vance. *High Flight: Aviation and the Canadian Imagination* (Toronto: Penguin Canada, 2002), 131.

106 *Nanaimo Daily News*. 5 March 1940, 3.

107 *The Windsor Star*. 21 March 1940.

108 *The Windsor Star*. 25 April 1940.

109 *The Windsor Star*. 25 April 1940, 26.

110 *The Windsor Star*. 14 May 1940, 11.

111 *The Windsor Star*. 14 May 1940, 11.

112 *Montreal Gazette*. 4 March 1942.

113 *Ottawa Journal*. 12 March 1942.

114 *Montreal Gazette*. 11 March 1942.

115 *Montreal Gazette*. 18 June 1928, 16.

BIBLIOGRAPHY
AND SOURCES

207 Squadron Royal Air Force History: World War I. www.207squadron. rafinfo.org.uk

The Aerodrome. www.theaerodrome.com

Bartlett, Nick. *In the Teeth of the Wind: Memoirs of the Royal Naval Air Service in the First World War.* London: Lee Cooper Publishers, 2013.

Bechthold, Mike. *Flying to Victory: Raymond Collishaw and the Western Desert Campaign, 1940-1941.* Norman, OK: Oklahoma University Press. 2017.

———. "Vimy and the Battle of Arras: The Evolution of the Air Campaign," *Journal of Military and Strategic Studies.* 2017. V18. Issue 2: 66.

Bennett, Allan D. *Captain Roy Brown: A True Story of the Great War, 1914-1918.* New York: Brick Tower Press, 2012, and iBooks, 2014.

Bewsher, Paul, RNAS. *The Dawn Patrol and Other Poems of an Aviator.* London: Erskine Macdonald Ltd., 1917.

———. *The Bombing of Bruges.* London: Hodder and Stoughton, 1918.

———. *Green Balls: The Adventures of a Night Bomber.* London: William Black and Sons, 1919.

Bishop, William Avery. *Winged Warfare.* Toronto: McClelland, Goodchild, and Stewart Publishers, 1918, and Toronto: McArthur and Company, 2002.

The British War in the Air 1914-1918. 3 October 1918 - Collisions. www. airwar19141918.wordpress.com.

Brown, Athol Sutherland. "Aces and the Development of Aerial Combat in the First World War on the Western Front," *The Journal of the Canadian Aviation Historical Society.* Summer 2014: 66-93.

Burt, Graham. "To E.A., Wife, Family, Cat, Chickens, etc.," *The Ontarion.* 11 November 2019.

Butts, Ed. "Ace flyer Playford Hales loved the sport of aerial dogfights," *Guelph Mercury*. 29 December 2014.

Canada, *Imperial War Service Gratuities 1919-1921*.

Canadian Forces College. "Early Aviation Heritage at Armour Heights." www. cfc.forces.gc.ca.

Canadian Museum of Flight. *Joseph Fall*. www.canadianflight.org/content/ gc-joseph-fall.

Cole, Christopher, ed. *Royal Air Force Communiques 1918*. London: Tom Donovan Publishers, 1990.

Commonwealth War Graves Commission. "Fort Worth Greenwood Memorial Park," "Arras Flying Services Memorial."

Cox, Sebastian. "Aspects of Anglo-US Co-operation in the Air in the First World War," *Air and Space Power Journal*. Winter 2004.

Curtiss, Glenn H., and Augustus Post. *The Curtiss Aviation Book*. New York: Frederick A. Stokes Co., 1912.

Deseronto Archives. J. Allan Smith Royal Flying Corps Training Camps Collection.

Dickson, Paul. "The Crerar's of Hamilton: A Study of Two Scottish Immigrants," *Scottish Tradition*, Vol XIX, 1994.

———. "Stinson, Marion Elizabeth (Crerar)" *Dictionary of Canadian Biography*, vol. 14. University of Toronto/Universite Laval, 1998. www.biographi.ca/ en/bio/stinson_marion_elizabeth_14E.html.

Dodds, Ronald. *The Brave Young Wings*. Stittsville, ON: Canada's Wings, 1980.

Douglas, W.A.B. "Archives and Canada's Official Air Force history," *Archivaria*. V26, Summer 1988.

Ellis, Frank H. *Canada's Flying Heritage*. Toronto: University of Toronto Press, 1968.

Franks, Norman, et al. *Black September 1918: WWI's Darkest Month in the Air*. London: Grub Street Press, 1918.

Franks, Norman. *Great War Fighter Aces 1916-1918*. London: Pen and Sword Aviation, 2017.

Gadd, Ronald. *Combat Stress Reactions and Morale in RFC/RAF Aircrew 1914-1918*. PhD thesis. University of Wolverhampton, 2020.

Gillis, Jocelyn. May 8, 1918. "Lieutenant Roderick McDonald." *Antigonish Cenotaph Project, Antigonish Heritage Museum*. 2008. https://antigonish cenotaphproject.wordpress.com/2018/05/08/may-8-1918-lieutenant-roderick-macdonald/.

Goodfellow, Sampson J. *One Lucky Devil: The First World War Memoirs of Sampson J. Goodfellow*. Edited by Edward Willett. Regina: Shadowpaw Press, 2018.

Gunn, Roger. *Raymond Collishaw and the Black Flight*. Toronto: Dundurn Press, 2013.

Guttman, Jon. *Naval Aces of World War I, Part I*. Oxford: Osprey Publishing, 2011.

———. "Bob Leckie: Zeppelin Strafer," *Esprit de Corps*. 12 July 2017. Vol 24-05.

Halliday, Hugh A., and Dr. Laura Brandon. "Into the Blue: Pilot Training in Canada, 1917–18." *Dispatches: Backgrounders in Canadian Military History*. Canadian War Museum.

Hartney, Lieut.- Col. Harold Evans. *Up and At 'Em: The War Memoirs of an American Ace*. Auckland, New Zealand: Pickle Partners Publishing. www. pp-publishing.com.

Henderson's City of Vancouver Directory 1907.

Hobbs, David. *The Royal Navy's Air Service in the Great War*. Barnsley, Yorkshire: Seaforth Publishing, 2017.

Hunt, C.W. *Dancing in the Sky: The Royal Flying Corps in Canada*. Toronto: Dundurn Press, 2009.

Hunt, P.W. *Handley Page O/400. Night Bomber Pilot. "A Brave Aviator and a Gentleman. A Short History*. Falls Church, VA: C.G. and P.V. Hint, 2017.

Imperial War Museum. *Training Pilots for the Imperial British Royal Flying Corps*. www.iwm.org.uk/collections/item/object/1060023299. This film shows the IRFC, particularly No. 4 SMA at the University of Toronto. Flying scenes appear to be Camp Borden.

Jackson, Robert. *101 Great Fighters*. New York: Rosen Publishing, 2010.

Jones, Paul Fortier. "Training to Fly and Fight," *Century Magazine*. September 1918: 681.

Joost, Mathias. "The Royal Flying Corps – Canada in Winter," *Canadian Aviation Historical Society Journal*. 50-3 Fall 2012: 96–101.

Kealy, J.D.F., and E.C. Russell. *A History of Canadian Naval Aviation 1918–1962*. The Naval Historical Section, Canadian Forces Headquarters, Department of National Defence. Ottawa, 1965.

Langley, John G. *Casey: The Remarkable Untold Story of Frederick Walker "Casey" Baldwin*. Halifax: Nimbus Publishing, 2019.

Libby, Frederick. *Horses Don't Fly: A Memoir of World War I*. Edited by Sally Marsh. New York: Arcade Publishing, 2000.

Lomas, Janis. "Delicate Duties: issues of class and respectability in government policy towards the wives and widows of British soldiers in the era of the Great War," *Women's History Review*, Volume 9, Number 1, 2000: 123.

Mackinnon, Gordon. "Lester Bowles "Mike" Pearson and the IRFC," *The Maple Leaf*. V24, 2012.

Macmillan, Norman. *Into the Blue*. London: Duckworth, 1929. London: Grub Street Press, 2015 (reprint).

"Major military awards of World War I: VC to MID," *The Gazette*. London. www.thegazette.co.uk/awards-and-accreditation/medals.

Male, Chris. *A Short History of the Royal Aeronautical Society: Part I, the Early Years*. www.aerosociety.com.

March, Bill. "A brief timeline of military aviation training in Canada," www. rcaf-arc.forces.gc.ca.

Maritime Archaeology Trust. "First World War Seaplane Stations of the South Coast of England," *Forgotten Wrecks of the First World War*. MAC. July 2018.

Marr, Douglas. "Naval 8 WWI," *Naval 8-208 Squadron History*. www. naval8-208-association.com.

Marsden, Barry M. *Camel Pilot Ace: The Great War Flying Career of Edwin Swale*. Barnsley, Yorkshire: Pen and Sword Aviation, 2017.

McCudden, James. *Flying Fury: Five Years in the Royal Flying Corps*. Philadelphia: Casemate, 2009.

McCurdy, J.A.D. *Deposition by J.A.D. McCurdy, April 9, 1920. MSS1268*. Library of Congress. Washington. www.loc.gov/resource/magbell. 14410301.

McGill Honour Roll 1914–18. McGill University. Montreal, 1926.

Milberry, Larry. "Aviation in Canada: How it all began," *Skies Magazine*. 23 February 2017.

Molkentin, Michael. "The Dominion of the Air: The Imperial dimension of Britain's war in the air, 1914-1918," *British Journal of Military History*. www.bjmh.org.uk.

Morley, Robert M. *Earning Their Wings: British Pilot Training 1912–1918*. Thesis. University of Saskatchewan, 2006.

Morton, Desmond, and Glen Wright. "The Bonus Campaign, 1919–1921: Veterans and the Campaign for Re-establishment," *Canadian Historical Review*. LXIV, 2, 1983.

Napier, Michael. *Winged Crusaders: The Exploits of 14 Squadron RFC and RAF 1915–1945*. Barnsley, Yorkshire: Pen and Sword Aviation. 2012.

Ontario Agricultural College Review. "The Late Captain J. Playford Hales." Vol. 32, No. 1. September 1919: 36.

Phillips, Glen C. *The Ontario Photographer List, Vol. II*. London, ON: Iron Gate Publishing, 1987.

Pitchfork, Graham. *Forever Vigilant: Naval 8/208 Squadron RAF. A Century of Service from 1916 to 2016*. London: Grub Street Publishing, 2016.

Price, Harold. "Diary." In *A Rattle of Pebbles: The First World War Diaries of Two Canadian Airmen*. Edited by Brereton Greenhous. Ottawa: Canadian Government Publication Centre 1997.

RAF Museum. *Story Vault*. Casualty Cards.

Ripon, T.S., and E.G. Manuel. "The Essential Characteristics of Successful and Unsuccessful Aviators, with Special Reference to Temperament," *The Lancet*. September 1918.

Rosenthal, Lyndsay. "New Battlegrounds: Treating VD in Belgium and Germany, 1918-19," in *Canada 1919: A Nation Shaped by War*. Edited by Tim Cook and J.L Granatstein. Vancouver: UBC Press, 2020.

Royal Aero Club Aviator's Certificates, 1910-1950. www.Ancestry.ca.

Russell, Ronda D. "Canada's Airmen and Airwomen in the First World War," *Airforce*, Summer 2004.

Semple, Clive. *Diary of a Night Bomber Pilot in World War I*. Edited by Alan Mawby. Stroud, UK: The History Press. 2008.

Shores, Christopher, Norman Franks, and Russell Guest. *Above the Trenches: A Complete Record of the Fighter Aces and Units of the British Empire Air Forces, 1915-1920*. London: Grub Street Press, 1990.

A Short History of 208 Squadron. www.naval8-208-association.com.

Snowie, J Allan. *Collishaw and Company: Canadians in the Royal Naval Air Service 1914-1918*. Bellingham, WA: Nieuport Publishing Inc., 2010.

Springs, Elliott White. *War Birds: A Diary of a Great War Pilot*. London: John Hamilton. 1927. And Mark Hillier ed. Barnsley, Yorkshire: Frontline Books, 2016.

Statistics Canada. "Prices of a family budget of staple foods, fuel and lighting, and rent, for 60 cities in Canada, 1920, 1926, and 1928 to 1936." *Canada Year Book, 1937*.

Strange, L.A. *Recollections of an Airman*. Havertown, PA: Casemate Publishers, 1933, 2016.

Sullivan, Alan. *Aviation in Canada, 1917-1918*. Toronto: Rous and Mann, 1919.

Surtees, Laurence. "Bell, Alexander Graham," *Dictionary of Canadian Biography*, vol. 15. University of Toronto/Universite Laval, 2005.

Taylor, Stewart K. "Impatient Ace: Charles Robert Reeves Hickey, DFC," *Cross and Cockade International*, Spring 2015. 46.044.

——. "John Roy Allan – Handley-Page Pilot," *The Journal of the Canadian Aviation Historical Society*. Vol. 34, No. 3, 1996.

——. "Naval's Bad Boy: FSL Arthur McBurney Walton, A Flight, 6 Squadron RNAS 1917," *Cross and Cockade International*. 38/3 2007.

———. "Sheer grit and fortitude: Oliver Joseph Gagnier, 6 Squadron, RNAS, 1917," *Cross and Cockade International*. 48/3, 2017.

———. "Two B******, FSL Alexander Richard 'Noisy' Knight and FSL Roderick 'Rod' McDonald. B Flight, Naval 8, 1917." *Cross and Cockade International*. 51.075 2020.

University of Toronto Roll of Service 1914-1918. Toronto: University of Toronto Press, 1921.

Vee, Roger. *Flying Minnows: Memoirs of a World War One Fighter Pilot; From Training in Canada to the Front Line, 1917-1918*. London: J. Hamilton, 1935; London: Arms and Armour Press, 1977.

Veterans Affairs Canada. *Canadian Virtual War Memorial*.

Warner, Guy. "Canadians at Felixstowe in the First World War," *CAHS Journal*. Spring 2014: 6-15.

Wansbrough, M.B. *Echoes That Remain: Highfield School History*. Hamilton: Highfield-Strathallan College, 2001.

Westrop, Mike. *A History of No. 6 Squadron, Royal Naval Air Service*. Artglen PA: Schiffer Publishing, 2006.

Wilkins, Mark C. *Aero-neurosis: Pilots of the First World War and the Psychological Legacies of Combat*. Philadelphia: Pen and Sword Aviation, 2019.

Williams, George K. *"Biplanes and Bombsights" British Bombing in World War I*. Maxwell Air Force Base, Alabama: Air University Press, 1999.

Wise, Sydney F. *Canadian Airmen and the First World War: The Official History of the RCAF. Vol. 1*. Toronto: University of Toronto Press, 1980.

Zeitlin, Michael. "Faulkner and the Royal Air Force." *The Faulkner Journal*. Vol. 30, No. 1. Baltimore, MD: Johns Hopkins University Press, 2016.

Archival Records and Libraries

Archives and Special Collections, University of Guelph, ON:
    The OAC Review.
    Letters of John Playford Hales.
Archives of Ontario, Toronto.
Archives and Special Collections, University of Guelph, ON.
BC Archives. BC Birth Records, BC Marriage Registrations. Victoria BC.
Canada Census 1901, 1911, 1921.
Commonwealth War Graves Commission.

Library and Archives Canada, Ottawa:
  Personnel Records of the First World War.
  Curtiss School of Aviation fonds.
Library of Congress, Washington.
Library, Vancouver Island Military Museum, Nanaimo, BC.
Minnesota State Archives, Gale Family Library. Minneapolis, MN.
National Archives of the UK:
  ADM 273.
  Air 1.
  Air 27.
  Air 76.
RAF Museum Story Vault. Casualty Cards.
Royal Aero Club Aviator's Certificates, 1910–1950. www.Ancestry.ca.
Toronto Public Library.
US Border Crossing Records 1914, 1918, 1919.
US Census 1910, 1920, 1930, 1940.
US City Directories 1822-1995. St. Paul, MN. 1915.
City of Vancouver Archives.

Newspapers

Calgary Herald
Daily Telegram
Guelph *Mercury*
The London Gazette
Minneapolis Star Tribune
Nanaimo Daily News
Nanaimo Semi-Weekly Mail
Ottawa Citizen
The Province
Toronto *Star*
The Victoria Daily Times
The Vancouver Daily World
Victoria Times Colonist

Periodicals

CAHS Journal
Cross and Cockade International
The Ontarion. University of Guelph

Interviews

Doreen Gagnier O'Keefe, Courtenay, BC.

INDEX

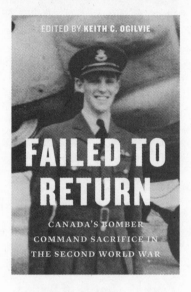

FAILED TO RETURN
Canada's Bomber Command Sacrifice in the Second World War

Keith C. Ogilvie (ed.)

"Of the 40,000 Canadians who served as aircrew in Bomber Command during the Second World War, almost 10,000 lost their lives. In its collection of portraits of some of these Canadians and their comrades in various crews lost, *Failed to Return* puts a human face to this statistic and helps ensure the memory of their sacrifice is not forgotten."

MARK ZUEHLKE
bestselling author of the *Canadian Battle Series*

ISBN 978-1-77203-381-6 (paperback)
ISBN 978-1-77203-382-3 (e-book)

THE SPITFIRE LUCK OF
SKEETS OGILVIE
From the Battle of Britain
to the Great Escape

Keith C. Ogilvie

"This is more than just a typical family history—this is
the remarkable story of a very lucky man, one who
took part in the aerial fight for England, who had to bale
out when his aircraft was shot down, was captured by the
Germans and endured years in prisoner-of-war camps—
and to top it off, was one of the few survivors of the famous
Great Escape. Highly readable and highly moving."

DAVE OBEE
Editor-in-Chief, Victoria *Times Colonist*

ISBN 978-1-77203-211-6 (paperback)